BEYOND CHAOS

FOREWORD BY ZIG ZIGLAR

BEYOND CHAOS

*Stress Relief
for the
Working Woman*

SHEILA WEST

NAVPRESS ●®
A MINISTRY OF THE NAVIGATORS
P.O. BOX 6000, COLORADO SPRINGS, COLORADO 80934

The Navigators is an international Christian organization. Jesus Christ gave His followers the Great Commission to go and make disciples (Matthew 28:19). The aim of The Navigators is to help fulfill that commission by multiplying laborers for Christ in every nation.

NavPress is the publishing ministry of The Navigators. NavPress publications are tools to help Christians grow. Although publications alone cannot make disciples or change lives, they can help believers learn biblical discipleship, and apply what they learn to their lives and ministries.

Printed in the United States of America

To my three most cherished "reasons for being":
my dearly beloved husband and partner, John, and
our precious children, Terri and John III.
And
to the loving memory of
Peg Haddad:
a woman of vision,
a legacy of love.

CONTENTS

AUTHOR

Sheila West started a business with her husband in 1981 after eighteen years as a homemaker.

Their entrepreneurial venture began as a 20' × 24' retail store and grew into a multi-company corporation, ACI Consolidated, Inc., of which Sheila is President and Chief Executive Officer. One of her companies, Archery Center International, has twice been named to the *INC.* 500 list of America's fastest-growing, privately-owned companies. Sheila has been nationally recognized for her business achievements, including the 1990 Michigan Emerging Entrepreneur of the Year awarded by Ernst & Young, Merrill Lynch, and *INC.* magazine. Additionally, she has been profiled in *INC.*, *USA Today*, Tom Peters' *On Achieving Success*, and several leading Christian publications.

A frequent speaker to corporations, business associations, and religious groups, Sheila has earned a nationwide reputation for commitment to personal growth and professional development. She utilizes fifteen years of public speaking experience to share the dynamics of excellence in everyday living through seminars, conferences, and retreats.

Sheila and her husband, John, live in Monroe, Michigan.

9

They have two grown children: Terri, who is married to Don Suhadolnik; and John III. Sheila is also a boating enthusiast, an avid walker, and a determined novice golfer.

FOREWORD

From time to time we encounter someone who is truly a difference-maker, one who has a positive impact not only on family, friends, and business associates, but on people all over the country. Such a person is Sheila West.

For eighteen years she carefully learned the tools of her trade. She functioned as the chief operating officer, prime decision-maker, chief financial officer, educator, custodian, nurse, and chef of the West household. Then one day she realized that her first assignment had been completed; she felt God had other assignments for her. With this in mind, she and her husband, John, started searching for the "right" opportunity. They looked at many different opportunities and ended up in the archery business.

From the chief operating officer of a small family to the chief executive officer of a large company seems like a giant step, and it is. But when you've built your life on a foundation of love, faith, and integrity, you're off to a good, solid start and can move from where you are to where you want to go. That's the position in which Sheila found herself. She shares the how-tos and exciting steps and procedures in this marvelous book, *Beyond Chaos*.

11

Did she make any mistakes? Are you kidding? Would she do some things differently if she were to start over? Maybe. But maybe not. If she had done them differently, she might not have ended up where she is. Sheila believes Romans 8:28, which says all things work together for good to those who love God, who serve Him according to His purpose. Some "bad" things happened to her and John along the way to where they are, but God took bad things and turned them to good.

Basically, the message Sheila delivers in her book is one of faith, hope, love, and encouragement. When you get through reading it, you'll feel better about yourself, more excited about your future, more grateful for those you love, and more enthusiastic about your faith. I love the eloquently simple expression Sheila uses: "Christianity should not glare, but it should glow." And you can see the glow throughout the book. Not an overt, beat-you-over-the-head-with-the-Bible approach, but the solid assurance that the God Sheila worships is One who concentrates on feeding the sheep, not on beating the sheep.

The thing I love about Sheila West is the fact that what she is writing about is totally consistent with the way she lives her life. You get the distinct impression that here is a servant of God who loves Him and tries to represent Him to the extent of her human ability. Here's a woman who loves her husband and fulfills the biblical role of wife and mother, while at the same time serving as a marvelous role model for those people who grow discouraged because of all the demands, chaos, and turmoil that exist in our society.

Here's a book with some encouraging, solid, common-sense procedures and instructions wrapped up in inspiration so that not only will you know what you ought to do, but you will know how to do it. I'm excited about the message in the book because I'm excited about the messenger who wrote the book. Not only will you find it easy, pleasant reading, but you will find it can well be a life-changing experience.

Beyond Chaos is a book by a woman about women and for women. Don't be confused by that sentence because the men who read this book will know more about what women really want, what women really expect, and how to not only live with them and love them, but to work with them in a far more effective way. It's my belief that this book will open the lines of communication between husbands and wives at home and men and women in the marketplace, enabling all of us to fulfill our roles in a more effective way. Congratulations, Sheila. I believe God is smiling and saying, "Well done, thou good and faithful servant."

— Zig Ziglar

PREFACE:
RIDING THE TIDES

I always enjoy watching surfers who challenge the big waves. I'm amazed at their skill in anticipating the incoming breakers and making snap decisions on the right one to ride. Even more impressive is their exceptional ability to get up and try again after a wave overcomes them.

Actually, surfers don't "ride" waves; they move with them. They work constantly to respond to the wave's changing movement. They must anticipate where the waves are going to break, adjust their movements for just the right response, and then follow it through once they've made their choice. They can't take anything for granted, or they'll get pulled under.

As working women in today's marketplace, we have something in common with the surfer out on the ocean: the experience can be exhilarating as well as exhausting. Whether or not we can move with the ever-changing tides depends on how keenly aware we are of the elements around us, how we adjust our responses accordingly, and whether we can persevere when the going gets tough.

There is one big difference, however: surfers have one area of concentration; we have many. The difficulty of trying to do or have it all can make us feel as if we're about to be pulled under. We look around at others and notice their composed exteriors — a presentation of order and control. *How do they do it?* we mutter under our breath. Beneath our own surface activity of busyness, we wonder how long we can keep going like this.

I think most working women — whether temporarily, seasonally, or regularly — struggle with this defeating feeling of "I just can't do it all! I can't keep up!"

I know I've felt this way, and not just when times were hard. Even career "success" doesn't take away the fundamental difficulty of meeting conflicting demands and living *in* control instead of *out* of control.

I wrote this book because I discovered that *career* and *chaos* don't have to be synonymous. There are alternatives to trying to have it all — *all at once.*

In the search for solutions we can get ourselves into a "cram management" mode. We separate our agendas into individual pieces and then try to figure out the key to the puzzle — how to make them all fit together in one "balanced" picture.

Beyond Chaos addresses these issues of multiple demands in the life of working women. Chaos is a condition of our environment, but it doesn't have to be a controlling factor in our lives. The agonizing sense of failure that comes from trying to "balance" our lives — as we always come up short — doesn't have to keep us hostage from what we want to accomplish and become.

In order to make the right responses to the changing environment we're in, we need to merge all of our agendas in a synchronized lifestyle that gives us flexibility to move ahead in increments of progress that vary from one agenda to the next. We need freedom to move in a way that allows us to focus on one thing at a time without being crowded by all the other things we're *not* doing at the moment — yet with the confidence that we aren't leaving everything else behind.

This book is all about disarming guilt trips and conflicting demands with a foundational "reason for being" that gives meaning to seemingly meaningless situations. Here is the starting point for the synchronized, flexible lifestyle I described above.

It's not the solution for those who are searching for a "quick fix"; it's the beginning of the answer for those who seek quality of life. It's the way to take charge and direct our ride along the tides of daily living.

These next eleven chapters are designed to instruct and inspire you in the art of purposeful living. Once you catch this wave, you'll share the exhilarating sensation of making the right moves at the right times. Even if you get pulled under, it will be only momentarily. You'll be able to bounce back up and climb aboard the right opportunities one more time.

We can't have it all, all at once. But we can fulfill our purpose—day by day, step by step—and enjoy the process. We can find meaning *beyond chaos*. May this become *your* experience as you read this book.

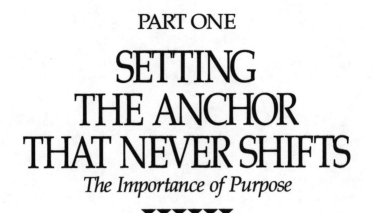

PART ONE

SETTING
THE ANCHOR
THAT NEVER SHIFTS
The Importance of Purpose

CHAPTER ONE

TAKE HOLD OF
SOMETHING INCREDIBLE

▼▼▼▼▼▼

Choice, not chance, determines destiny.[1]

The refreshing breeze of early evening didn't cool me off as I locked the office door at the end of a long work day.

I was boiling inside. Here I was the last one to leave work — yet they were paging me from home wanting to know when dinner would be ready.

I didn't feel like cooking dinner. At that point, I didn't even feel like going home. All I wanted to do was get in the car and just keep driving.

I switched on the radio to drown out my negative thoughts — just in time to hear: . . . *there are those of you who are frustrated, depressed, disillusioned, and discouraged. All you want to do is run.* . . .

I was shocked to hear this strange voice describing my innermost feelings. He went on: . . . *there are mothers who are distraught, spouses who are disillusioned, business people who are discouraged.* . . . That was *me* he was talking about. I was a mother, a spouse, a CEO of a young and fast-growing company: and I felt that the stress of trying to do it all was pulling me apart.

Then the voice on the radio delivered the punchline that really hit home: . . . *you may be asking, "What is the purpose?"*

21

And was I ever. Why did my business success seem so meaningless and empty? Where had all the joy gone, the sense of accomplishment?

REELING FROM THE REAL WORLD

Once I stopped to think about it, I realized my whole world was reeling. I was sure that whoever had told the woman of the eighties she could do it all had never tried to do it themselves. I felt like I was running inside. Overwhelming demands to meet urgent needs shouted at me until my mind raced with fear that I would leave something undone.

I just can't keep this up anymore, I thought to myself. My compulsion to be "strong," to live up to the "I can handle anything" image, was crumbling before a growing desire to be taken care of. I longed to be a beacon in the marketplace, but I ached with a sense of failure as daily pressures sapped my energy. This little light of mine seemed to get dimmer every day.

Now, as I look back on that crisis of purpose, I realize that I was probably only one of millions of women struggling on the stormy seas of career challenges. But at that moment I thought no one understood or cared. In my isolation, my only answer to "What's the purpose?" was "Just survive!"

Yet even in my tailspin, I knew that there was more purpose for me in the marketplace than just survival. Deep down, I felt that something was out of sync. There had to be a reason why the real world had set me reeling. But what was it?

A MID-LIFE CHANGE

I started on a process of searching for answers to my surprise attack of meaninglessness. Why the frustration, the anger, the fear? Why would the CEO of one of America's successful young companies feel her life just wasn't working?

My life had shifted gears to the fast track a year earlier. For eighteen years I'd been in the catering business—"catering" to a husband, two children, and Pepi, a hyperactive poodle. During that period I'd been developing some ideas for the next phase of my life. I was determined not to be a victim of the "empty vision" syndrome—being blind-sighted by life's never-ending changes, especially once the children no longer needed constant attention.

While I was preparing for the changes to come, my husband came down with an attack of 40-40 vision. This condition forces the questions, "What have I accomplished in my first forty years? And what do I want to do with my next forty years?" Together, he and I decided to focus our efforts on making the transition through mid-life fulfilling by becoming partners in our own business. We began a cautious search for the right opportunity.

Although I was a little apprehensive, I felt the situation was under control—until that day when John came home from work with a mischievous smile playing across his lips and said, "Honey, let's buy a bow shop."

"Say what?" I stuttered.

"A *bow shop*," he responded. "You know—archery equipment!"

My mind raced to a vision of the paraphernalia that cluttered our family room on days when his friends came over to shoot their bows.

"Are you kidding?" I asked in alarm. Bows and arrows were toys, not a serious business opportunity.

"C'mon, where's your sense of adventure?" John prodded.

At this point I realized my husband wasn't joking. He really wanted us to go into business selling bows and arrows!

For the next few days, I kept up an internal dialogue with myself. Archery equipment hadn't been on my list of acceptable business ventures. But in all honesty, the challenge was beginning to appeal to me.

As John and I went through a careful process of analysis and research, the vision for the bow shop started coming together. Four months later, potential became reality with the opening of The Archery Center, with me at its helm full-time.

In its first year, The Archery Center grew more rapidly than any of us had expected. But the early success of our business took its toll on me. The learning curve I zoomed onto was dizzyingly steep. Changes came fast and furious, and with them a multitude of demands. No wonder that at the end of that first year I was reeling from my plunge into "the real world."

WHY THE CHAOS?

Now that I'm an experienced businesswoman, I realize how green I was in those early days. The personal and professional changes were mind-boggling. The business skills and technical knowledge I had to acquire overnight seemed insurmountable. The family commitments and sacrifices were never-ending. And the benefits seemed hidden behind the bills.

My search for answers to my crisis turned up some explanations. I had been trying to juggle multiple roles without any understanding of how to resolve the inevitable conflicts. I was spreading myself thinner all the time, trying to do it all, without any clear system of priorities. *I was caught in a chaotic lifestyle without any method for organizing the chaos.*

In my experience as a CEO and a frequent speaker to women's groups, religious as well as business and professional, I've discovered that this sense of "what's it all about?" is the experience of many of today's women in the marketplace. Buffeted by constant waves of conflicting demands or unmet expectations, women are suffering from a crisis of meaning and purpose.

Why the chaos? Here are some explanations from my own experience and the stories of countless women I've counseled.

1. *Women feel that as much as they do, it's never enough.* Many women are staggering under a load of guilt and self-doubt. They feel weighed down by the need to give primary attention and energy to all areas of their life at once. When they can't perform this miraculous feat, they feel defeated, helpless to keep all the balls in the air at the same time. The conflicting demands continue to pull them back and forth until they're reeling in confusion, with no real sense of where they're heading.

The resulting guilt and frustration keeps women from enjoying or feeling satisfaction in the contributions they *are* making. They mistakenly assume that they have to give equal priority to all areas of their lives. If they emphasize one particular responsibility, they feel guilty about "neglecting" the others. And so they're caught in a trap of trying to "balance" family, work, relationships, personal health, career growth, and so on.

But the balancing act doesn't work. And so the guilt and fatigue increase until the chaos seems overwhelming.

2. *Women are unprepared for the cultural shock of entering the marketplace.* Whether they're leaving behind college life, time out of the work world to raise young children, or a homemaking career, many women face major adjustments when entering or reentering the marketplace.

Trading in the familiar for the unfamiliar is always difficult. But when women leave an environment with well-defined boundaries and structured expectations for a mega-marketplace powered by a highly competitive drive and colored with a dizzying array of values, beliefs, and alternative lifestyles, they can suffer serious culture shock. Webster's defines this condition as "a sense of confusion and uncertainty, sometimes with feelings of anxiety, that may affect people exposed to alien culture without adequate preparation."[2] Amen.

It takes time and experience to identify those unwritten, unspoken rules that shape the society of the marketplace. It's hard work to deal with the constant bombardment of conflicting work ethics, various personalities, and differing energy levels. Adding to these difficulties are the social norm deregulations of recent decades. It's extremely challenging for women and men who grew up in a structured society to simply define new roles for themselves in a changing business culture. So even after women merge into the business mainstream, they must grapple with uncertainty regarding what is expected of their contribution.

Christian women especially struggle with these issues in light of the values and beliefs of their faith. They wrestle in applying God's guidelines to on-the-job challenges. They confront religious agendas warning them not to overstep specific boundaries. They wonder how to be a clear light in a world of complex pressures.

The clamor of many voices can be pandemonium in the ears of today's working woman.

3. *Exhaustion from keeping up with demands makes women fear that there's no real purpose behind the sacrifices they're making.* Most of us thrive on worthwhile work. But when we begin feeling that all of our hard struggle is for nothing, the chaos of the daily grind can become unbearable.

In her book *Gift from the Sea,* Anne Morrow Lindbergh points out that women need to know there are good reasons for giving themselves:

> Here is a strange paradox. Woman instinctively wants to give, yet resents giving herself in small pieces. Basically is this a conflict? Or is it an over-simplification of a many-stranded problem? I believe that what woman resents is not so much giving herself in pieces as giving herself purposelessly. What we fear is not so much that our energy may be leaking away through small outlets as that it may be going "down the drain". . . .
>
> Purposeful giving is not as apt to deplete one's resources; it belongs to that natural order of giving that seems to renew itself even in the act of depletion.[3]

The shout from today's marketplace echoes these feelings. The woman of the nineties is saying, "Yes—give me work, but make it purposeful! Give me a place on the cutting edge, but don't cut me into bits and pieces!"

Yet most women live without a sense of purpose that guides them through the demands of the working world. I asked Denise, a single parent with a responsible position in a national corporation, "What's your purpose?" She responded, "I wish I knew. It's what I'm always looking for—my purpose and my place. But most of the time, I only discover it in hindsight."

True purpose isn't a product of hindsight, and it isn't developed in the moment of crisis. It's what empowers us to go forward and guides us along our journey. Therefore, it's tremendously important that we stop looking for our *place* in the working world and start understanding our *purpose* as working women. This understanding is what will clear a way through the chaos of our busy lives.

FINDING OUR PURPOSE IN LIFE

How easy it is to lose all sense of direction when we're pushed by the distractions and responsibilities of our job from one side; squeezed by the demands on our time from another side; and caught off-guard by confrontations with family from the inside.

Chaos is disorienting. But it needn't be defeating. The question for us is not *whether we will experience chaos* — because this side of Heaven it's guaranteed — but *how we will respond to it.*

It's the same situation with purpose. The dilemma is not *if* you will be confronted with the question of your purpose in life and work; it's when, how hard the question will hit, and whether or not you will be prepared to answer it. Everyone has a purpose, but each of us must seek to become secure in it.

Purpose is the anchor that never shifts — it allows us to change direction without losing sight of our goal. When the chaos whispers that life no longer makes sense, *purpose is what gives meaning to a seemingly meaningless situation.* It gives us our bearings when we're drifting in confusion. It enables us to navigate through the chaos without getting pulled under.

How do we find our purpose in life? The answer is not in *where* we look, but in *who* we turn to.

In his letter to the Colossians, the Apostle Paul describes the foundation of our purpose:

> So then, just as you received Christ Jesus as Lord, continue to live in him, rooted and built up in him, strengthened in the faith as you were taught, and overflowing with thankfulness.
>
> See to it that no one takes you captive through hollow and deceptive philosophy, which depends on human tradition and the basic principles of this world rather than on Christ.[4]

Our constancy of purpose is rooted in our life in Christ. In its most fundamental form, *our purpose as working women is to be God's woman in the marketplace*. This is what gives us direction and meaning. It keeps us from being blown off course by the winds of the marketplace — the human traditions and basic principles of this world.

But staying rooted in Christ isn't easy when the demands of living threaten to pull our focus away to other priorities. When other voices are clamoring for our attention, we need to cut through the noise to a quiet place that gives us the opportunity to listen to God.

There's a dynamic passage in the Bible recording how God spoke to one of His prophets — a man very much in need of direction in the midst of chaos. I paraphrase it like this: There was a powerful wind of conflict, but the Lord was not in the wind. There were the unpredictable forces of the earthquake of adversity, but the Lord wasn't in the earthquake. There was the intensity of the fire of passion, but the Lord wasn't in the fire. And then came the gentle whisper — the Lord *was* there![5]

We, too, have the elements of conflicting schedules, unpredictable crises, and burning passions. But in the midst of chaos, we must be quiet enough to hear God. God *is* there — and so is His purpose for our lives.

How difficult it can be to hear God's whisper when we're surrounded with noisy distractions. Recently I had a chance to realize just how noisy my world is when I spent a couple of days at Glen Eyrie, a Christian retreat center in Colorado on the front range of the Rocky Mountains.

I have a deathly fear of snakes. I was out walking a trail along the foothills when a sudden noise on the ground nearby made me jump in fright. Holding my breath, I glanced back over my shoulder. But there was no menace lying in wait. In the quiet of the moment, I had simply heard the wind rustling through the grasses.

Listening for God's whisper requires quieting down long enough to train our ears to the sound of His voice. When we are not focusing on His life in us, we become disoriented. The winds of conflict, the earthshaking adversities, and the flames of passion can't give us stability in the midst of chaos — we can find it only in the constancy of purpose. Then we will see His power burst forth in our lives, using our potential to do what often seems impossible.

OUR ULTIMATE ROLE MODEL

God's foundational purpose for us, and what it means to be God's woman, becomes clearer when we look at Jesus — the One who stayed perfectly focused amid the upheaval of agonizing demands, expectations, and crises.

Jesus constantly made decisions based upon His purpose — to do the will of His Father. He demonstrated this integrity in the way He handled the chaos of life:

- ◆ He understood His agenda — "[The disciples] exclaimed: 'Everyone is looking for you!' Jesus replied, 'Let us go somewhere else . . . so I can preach there also. That is why I have come.'"[6]
- ◆ He had a clear vision of His purpose — "For God did not send his Son into the world to condemn the world, but to save the world through him."[7]
- ◆ He understood where His power came from — "I tell you the truth, the Son can do nothing by himself; he can do only what he sees his Father doing, because whatever the Father does the Son also does."[8]
- ◆ He directed His life toward pleasing God, not Himself — "I seek not to please myself but him who sent me."[9]
- ◆ His care for people empowered them to live fully — "I have come that they may have life, and have it to the full."[10]
- ◆ He did not turn from His purpose, even under extreme pressure — "Now my heart is troubled, and what shall I say? 'Father, save me from this hour'? No, it was for this very reason I came to this hour."[11]

What a pattern to follow — to move through the marketplace steadily attuned to God's desire for our lives, having a divine impact on the people and society of our time!

Sometimes we think of the Christian faith as requiring a "plain Jane" lifestyle. But there was nothing plain about Jesus' lifestyle. It was demanding, but fulfilling; exhausting, but exhilarating; spontaneous, but structured. That was because Jesus stayed focused on His purpose even through the worst of the chaos around Him.

Jesus was rejuvenated by doing His Father's will. And He has promised to be not only our example, but our enabler, as we let Him live in us. *The strength that He provides is our guarantee that we will be able to live in the constancy of His purpose for us.*

PURPOSE IN THREE DIMENSIONS

But how do we bring this lofty purpose down to earth? Many of us find it difficult to envision what it really looks like to be God's woman in the marketplace.

Psychologists tell us that we think in pictures. But the first time I tried to develop a visual concept of my purpose, all I could picture was trying to survive.

What helps me now is to visualize three dimensions of purpose: *created, guiding,* and *driving.* Each of these aspects is distinct, yet they must be understood together in order to get a clear image of the value of being a purpose-empowered woman.

Created purpose refers to the reason why God created us — to become more like Him, reflecting Him in day-to-day living so that others will be drawn to Him as well. We know from Scripture that all of us have been created with this same purpose.

But God did not make us like so many robots on an assembly line. We're *individuals.* And therefore, God has customized a plan for each of us to carry out this purpose. We don't have to know the details of this plan — all we have to do is be responsive to Him each day in the choices we make. But more about that in later chapters.

To picture created purpose, think of some of the "givens" of

your life: you're a woman, a daughter. You were born with certain natural abilities that are suited to particular tasks and roles. The hand of God has painted a masterpiece—you—and destined you for a specific niche in His world that no one else can fill.

Isn't it a relief to know that you're not a chance happening? The purpose for which you've been created is yours and yours alone. Doesn't it give you a sense of stability to know that you are not just drifting along from birth to death singing "que será, será, whatever will be, will be"? You are here to make a contribution with eternal significance.

Too often the chaos creates such stress that we question if there's any meaning to all of it. This happens when we lose sight of our created purpose. To regain it, we need to turn to God once again to get our bearings and restore our faith that His plan for our lives is still in place.

Guiding purpose is the set of values, beliefs, and attitudes that provide the criteria for judging how to apply our created purpose to our life circumstances.

We always have a guiding purpose, but the direction it takes us in depends upon what we're setting our sights on in life. Guiding purpose is shaped by our intentions, our motives, our character. It can lead us into the shallow waters of selfish living or into the rich depths of having a positive impact on others.

What does guiding purpose look like? Imagine the "bigger picture" of the kind of person you want to become. What kinds of character traits do you want your life to reflect? What kind of influence do you want to have on others? This picture of your guiding purpose can be the pivot point for the choices you make along your journey. It will determine your motives and your methods; it will shape your attitudes and your behavior.

Guiding purpose carries created purpose into the choices that life sets before us. It provides standards that help us make effective decisions in the face of crossed signals and conflicting information. It gives us permission to say yes or no; it establishes a reference point for resolving conflicts. It springs from what we cultivate in our heart.

Driving purpose is what makes us get up out of bed in the

morning (no, I'm not talking about that first cup of coffee). It is the cluster of our needs in life—spiritual, physical, mental, emotional, social, financial.

We all have the same basic physiological needs, as well as common denominators in our needs for safety and security, love, self-esteem, etc. However, the particular mix of elements that drives each of us is individualized. What drives some people is not the same as what drives others. Some are motivated by competitiveness; others by an innate creativity. I might have a strong drive to empower others to reach their maximum potential; you might be drawn to caring for those with special needs.

I call this unique driving force that powers each of us our *passion of purpose*. This passion is the spice of life. You know when it's there and you know when it's missing. It's funny—we insist on it in our art, our music, and our sports, but not often enough in our work. Yet passion can bring forth our best effort. Internal zeal, not external applause, keeps us ignited when others are sputtering out. *The passion of purpose separates the movers and shakers from the moved and shaken.*

But the value of passion, like the value of fire, depends on how passion is used. When fire burns out of control, it destroys everything in its path. Those who passionately pursue their ambitions without regard for others are destructive forces in the marketplace. When fire is controlled and deliberately fed, it sheds warmth and light. Those who passionately pursue professional excellence and encourage others to do the same reflect a welcome glow in the marketplace.

THE ALIGNMENT PROBLEM

Purpose is the framework of life that enables us not only to *say* we desire to be God's woman in the marketplace, but to *become* God's woman. It keeps us from being crushed with failure and egotistical with success; it gives us the know-how to steer our way through tough decisions.

But in order for purpose to be the anchor that keeps us from drifting, its three dimensions must be aligned with each other. Created purpose forms the foundation—our reason to be; guiding purpose supplies the values by which we make choices—our reason for *how* we do what we do; driving purpose puts it all into action—the reason *why* we do what we do.

If we don't keep these three functioning in harmony, we begin to lose our effectiveness. We forget why we're on the journey; we compromise in order to take shortcuts to our goals; we are driven to get our needs met without considering what really gives meaning to our lives.

How do we know when our sense of purpose is out of alignment? First we need to have it well defined. In order to create a clear concept of my purpose so I would know when it was out of kilter, I did the same thing I'd done for my business: I wrote it out word for word. This brought home to me how vague my picture had been of what it means to be "God's woman in God's plan."

The process of writing this statement was just like creating a picture. I kept working with it over a period of time, shaping the wording to strengthen the connection between my passion of purpose and my day-to-day activities. As my purpose statement came into focus, it became the "why" that inspired the "how." I summarize it as "to become more like the Master and to make Him more meaningful in the marketplace." But I keep a longer version (see the appendix, "Creating a Personalized Plan," page 199) that functions like a cornerstone in establishing direction in each of my agendas.

Once I have a clear definition of purpose, enabling me to understand how it should be moving me forward without letting chaos pull me off course, I can recognize when the dimensions of purpose are out of alignment. Years ago I was doing the speed limit out on the expressway when my car began pulling to the left. I knew something was wrong but had no idea what it was. When John took it out for a test drive, he knew immediately that the front end was out of alignment. After that episode I never had to guess why the car seemed to be fighting my efforts to steer it. I knew it was an alignment problem.

The same is true with purpose. When its dimensions aren't in harmony, a pulling feeling starts. It may come from stretching the truth to get a new position; putting down someone else in the office to make ourselves look better; letting an office relationship become inappropriate. But whatever the cause, the result is always the same: the chaos is pulling us off-course.

To realign, we must stop and remember why we're here on earth—that is, our basic reason for living. We must review our values and beliefs to make sure they're built on the right bottom line. Then we need to be honest with ourselves about what's driving us and whether the methods we're using to get there are consistent with our values and beliefs. We need to ask ourselves, *Am I looking for my security in what I am driven to do, or in who God has created me to be?*

Once we've realigned our purpose—and we'll need to do this continually throughout our lifetime—we will be empowered once again to reach our maximum potential. We will be equipped to move through the chaotic demands of our lives with energy and confidence.

TAKING HOLD OF SOMETHING INCREDIBLE

In the next chapter we'll be talking about developing confidence in *your* understanding of what it means to be God's woman, marketplace style. If purpose supplies the paints we use to create a picture, then confidence is the tool we use to paint that vision of what we want to become. "Action-vision," which we'll explore in later chapters, is what empowers us to move toward this picture in the day-by-day, step-by-step process of purposeful living.

My deepest hope is that this book will inspire you to take hold of your purpose in life and to begin using the tools that will equip you to direct your life according to that purpose. Once you set out on this kind of journey, you'll find it will last a lifetime.

Recently, I found myself on the verge of a minor panic attack as I faced D-Day on an important deadline. As I was rushing (once again!) to complete some work, I was surprised by the arrival of a floral bouquet at my desk. The accompanying card, signed by my daughter, read, "Mom, it will go great. Just remember the Chill Pill! Love you, Terri."

Knowing how my Type-A personality flares up occasionally, Terri figured I'd be standing close to the ragged edge about now and sent me the flowers and note to calm and encourage me.

Taking the Chill Pill, as Terri and I refer to it, means remembering that Christ in me, and the constancy of purpose in Him, is my anchor in the midst of a chaotic marketplace. I find that reminding myself of this truth slows down the frequency of internal chaos and speeds up the realignment process.

Now I look back on that day at the office when I wanted to jump in my car and keep driving—away from the chaos, to find relief in a life that wasn't a jumble of conflicting demands and exhausting challenges—and I think about how far afield we travel in the search for a purpose that will make sense of our lives.

When we find that purpose, the feeling is that the straining engine of expectation has just shifted into the high gear of realization. It feels as if we're taking hold of something incredible—and we are! Because it's then, and only then, that we take hold of the truth that *being God's woman in God's plan is not a price to pay, but a priority to cherish.*

CHAPTER TWO

ADJUST YOUR OWN SAILS

▼▼▼▼▼

Trust in God. Believe in yourself.
Dare to dream.[1]

E*xpectations.* That word can conjure up exhilarating feelings when we're anticipating events such as college graduation, a joyful wedding, the job we've been waiting for, the first promotion.

But it can also lead to disappointment when our expectations aren't met or we feel we're coming up short in meeting someone else's.

Even after I began to grasp the concept of purpose, it seemed my emotions fluctuated from one end of the spectrum to the other. I had caught on quickly to how I could build on purpose professionally as the driving force of my business. This helped even out my roller coaster of expectations and produce purposeful accomplishments. Personally, however, I drifted all too long.

There was a gap between getting a handle on which to hang my "reason for being" and defining what it really meant to be "God's woman in God's plan" on a daily basis.

I was trying to work within a framework of being all things to all people, and it was making career and chaos synonymous. Going with the flow of regular demands was unleashing a flood of conflicting concepts about what I should or shouldn't be doing. I found myself constantly drifting from my desires to others' demands; from the joy of accomplishment to the stress of half-done or undone; from stimulating feelings to overwhelming frustrations.

It didn't make me feel any better to notice when I looked around the marketplace that others were in the same drifting mode. I had no exclusive on trying to do it all, all at the same time. Other women were feeling the fears of uncertainty, the pressures of meeting mammoth expectations, the panic of possible failure. All of us needed purpose to empower us to find our niche and stop second-guessing ourselves.

In a roundtable discussion I led at a conference, I saw all colors of the spectrum: the stay-at-home mother who had left career behind and faced reprimands for leaving the burden of financial support on her husband . . . the careerist who endured continual questions about being a full-time professional and a part-time mom . . . the mid-life returnee who was searching for herself . . . the single parent torn by guilt because she couldn't be it all. These were all different women, but they shared a common denominator: they were caught in the struggle between superwoman and suppressed woman.

Everywhere we turn, someone has an agenda for us: society's stereotypes, our friends' expectations, our employer's requirements, family assumptions, ideas in the Christian community about "biblical roles." We struggle to move forward without rocking anyone's boat.

How do we resolve this dilemma of *who* we should be and *what* we should be doing? I found that taking purpose beyond a general definition to a personal application gave me a framework that quickly laid conflicts to rest. It took a little work, but it gave me the confidence to use purpose to steer through the chaos of decision-making without being overcome by conflicting signals.

How freeing it is when we can answer these questions for ourselves: "What's really important to God, to me, and to those who are most affected by my choices? What desires, gifts, and abilities do I bring to the drawing board?" Then purpose becomes our criteria for making choices based on who we are and what we're trying to accomplish. We dig down for deeper issues than simply "to work or not to work"; we can turn our energies from defending our position to moving forward with our plans. Purpose becomes our tie-breaker when we're pulled in different directions; it leverages us into taking action on the right choices for our individual situation.

Once purpose became the motivating force in my choices, I was amazed at how much my commitment was formerly affected by the distractions of others dictating to me. My views of what I was trying to accomplish had been distorted; my agendas had been determined by the pressures of projects and people, not the passion of purpose.

Now I could see the great wisdom of the Apostle Paul in his confident proclamation that the God who began a good work in us would carry it through to completion.[2] How stress-relieving! Our purpose is based not on people's opinions, but on God's good work in us. We can have confidence in knowing that we are in process toward the certain accomplishment of God's will, even if it's not always according to our own expectations.

True freedom comes when we make choices according to how our purpose determines our direction — instead of trying to carve out agendas designed to obtain someone else's stamp of approval.

PURPOSE FREES US TO BE OURSELVES

One day while I was trying to visualize how purpose gives us meaning and direction in life, it occurred to me that purpose is also what gives us the freedom to be unique. I began connecting the function of purpose to the function of DNA, the genetic coding material.

DNA (*deoxyribonucleic acid*) is the chemical that stores, duplicates, and transmits the information that determines exactly how the billions of cells that make up the body come together. It creates the building blocks that ensure all human beings have the same basic characteristics but also that each human being will be a unique individual.

Our purpose has the same powerful components. We have all

been created with the same God-given purpose. Through Christ's life in us, we have stored within all the power and resources necessary to keep growing. On the other hand, God duplicates Christlikeness in each of us through different life experiences. As we fulfill individual roles, He transmits the same love of Christ through us.

We have all been created for Christ to live in us, to duplicate His Christlikeness in our lives, and to transmit His love through us to others . . . uniquely. That's powerful. We have the *security* of purpose—the constancy that determines our identity and forms the basis of our values and beliefs. But we also have the *freedom* of purpose—to live it out in our own individualized way.

Now let's look at how this concept of purpose as our DNA forms an acrostic that neatly summarizes the three dimensions of purpose:

Direction—from our created purpose;
Nature—from our guiding purpose;
Actions—from our driving purpose.

Created purpose determines our *direction* in life; guiding purpose determines our *nature* as we develop values and beliefs; and driving purpose determines our *actions* as we choose methods and agendas for pursuing our vision.

CONFIDENCE: OUR LEVERAGE FOR LIVING

Purposeful living is freeing because it's not our purpose to be perfect—yet. It is to be in process toward God's perfection. Everything we do, no matter what the results, works toward that ultimate goal when we're focused on our purpose.

But living in the freedom of being ourselves doesn't come easily. Some women are searching to redefine their purpose. Others have a clear sense of purpose, but lack the techniques to apply it to daily living.

Living in the confidence of our individualized purpose means pushing back the voices that want us to conform to their way of living. It requires going against our old patterns of performing for others in order to win their approval. It involves taking risks as we enter uncharted areas. And sometimes, it takes us places we'd rather not go—we prefer the old destinations because at least they're familiar to us.

The tool that equips us to act in the freedom of being ourselves is *confidence*. It enables us to push back the voices, to change old patterns, to take risks, to break through stereotypes. It's the inner strength we need to be consistent in pursuing our purpose through the challenges and strains of a hectic marketplace.

Think of how a lever can apply your effort and, by turning on a fulcrum point, lift a weight you could never move without such a tool. That's how confidence operates. As we make the effort to live out our customized purpose, it supplies the leverage we need to move heavy obstacles out of our way. It enables us to overcome our fears of inadequacy, our worries about what others will think of us, our caution in the face of the unknown.

Confidence is our leverage for living. But I'm not talking about simple pep talks and the power of positive thinking—helpful as those methods can be. I'm talking about something rooted deeper than ourselves, which is why we can count on it even in the worst attacks of self-doubt that life as a working woman can bring on us.

I learned early in my business career how important confidence is in order to achieve my goals as a working woman.

DITSY WOMAN OR BUSINESSWOMAN?

One of the requirements of entering the marketplace is convincing people that you're offering something of value. But I found out right away that you can't do this just by having the right qualifications or by being "nice."

My confidence was taking a beating every time a customer came into our shop and dismissed my offer of help by saying, "I'll wait until John gets here." After several months of this, I was totally frustrated. Ninety percent of our customers were men, and I felt sure they were thinking, "What's this ditsy woman doing in the archery business?"

I needed relief. Hoping that surrounding myself with something more familiar would boost my confidence, I decided to reorganize my closets at home. That's always been my frustration outlet. Compared to a day at work, it's soothing to immerse myself in the solitude of sorting through clothes, books, and trinkets.

On this particular closet-cleaning adventure, I happened upon my children's favorite story, *The Pony Engine*.[3] I hadn't read it in years, so I took a few moments to scan back through the book.

I reread the story of the train that broke down while taking children to the circus. In desperation, the circus train pleaded for help from other engines. First came a big, new engine who snorted, "I can't bother with you. I pull only the finest trains." Next came another train in need of repairs, moaning, "Give me reSSt! I've done E-nuff!" It was followed by a rusty, dusty engine grumbling, "I NEVER could! I NEVER could!"

The circus train was ready to give up when the pony engine, a very small train, pulled up alongside and said, "You're very heavy, and I'm not so big. But I will try. . . . I THINK I can!" It began pulling the circus train up the steep hills—slowly at first, but then gathering momentum as it huffed, "I THINK I can! I THINK I can!" Against all odds it succeeded, breezing downhill and tooting, "I THOUGHT I could! I THOUGHT I could!"

This children's story hit me between the ears. My brain cells finally started registering that my success in the marketplace wasn't being sabotaged by my customers' lack of confidence in me. It was being sabotaged by *my* lack of confidence in me! I was selling myself short, subconsciously declaring, "I think I CAN'T." I was questioning my own ability and deferring to John. No wonder my customers naturally gravitated toward him.

That insight brought home to me the truth of the saying, "If you really do put a small value upon yourself, rest assured that the world will not raise the price." I decided right then and there to change gears. Opportunity was knocking, but I needed confidence to open the door. I would never succeed unless I believed I could—and that meant not allowing others to dictate whether or not I was effective.

No more trying to sell others on myself by hiding self-doubt behind a smile, I determined. If I wanted others to have confidence in me, first I had to have it in myself.

FROM SELF-DOUBT TO CONFIDENCE

I'm not qualified to theorize about the psychological dynamics of how our confidence gets undermined. But my trek through the marketplace has convinced me that we *all* have those agonizing struggles with self-doubt. Even when I've been riding the current of success, I've been in situations in which I was so far away from where I was supposed to be that I needed mental binoculars just to keep the goal in sight.

When self-doubt threatens our progress, we need to hold on to the truth that we have a purpose and be confident that we can fulfill that purpose.

Now you're probably thinking, *But how can I feel confident about being able to fulfill my purpose when I'm suffering from self-doubt? That's what self-doubt is: lack of confidence!*

You're right—but the whole thing depends on how you understand confidence. If you think of it as just your own assessment of how well you perform, you'll lose it whenever circumstances aren't going your way. But if you think of it as an *attitude of expectation*, then self-doubt doesn't have the power to cancel it out.

Here's how I define it: *confidence is an attitude of faith that guides us from within.* It comes from believing that we are loved, that we have a purpose, and that in God's grace we are capable of fulfilling that purpose. It motivates us to accept challenge; it prevents fear from paralyzing us. Confidence as an attitude of expectation keeps us from putting our visions into the straitjacket of "See what happened last time?"

Why do we default to self-doubt? My guess is that we're

so busy trying to keep the wolves at bay—to put food on the table, to move forward in our careers, to maintain our homes, to keep up with relational demands—that the need for developing a good confidence flow is continually overridden by crisis management.

Doubts can be useful as a focusing tool to see where we really are. They can stimulate a self-awareness that leads to growth. But woe be unto us when self-doubt opens up an unbridgeable chasm between who we are and who we have the potential to be.

THE CHAOS WE CREATE: MIND GAMES

Confidence in who we are and what we're doing is crucial to our effectiveness as working women. But developing it takes discipline—the conscious effort to confront and deal honestly with our self-doubts. When we attempt to cover them up by ignoring them or just playing the part we think others expect of us, we create our own chaos. And we all know there's enough chaos in our lives that we can't get rid of—we don't need to heap more on top of it!

An attitude of expectation looks toward *potential*. But when we play subconscious mind games that undermine or tear down that potential, we sabotage our self-image—and sometimes our career as well.

Nicole was a very capable legal secretary. But she created her own crisis by allowing her mind games free rein. She was constantly second-guessing her ability and developing unfounded perceptions that every problem represented an attack on her.

Nicole answered the telephone one day and was surprised to hear her friend Ann on the other end. She listened with growing horror as Ann inquired about a secretarial position listed in the classified ads. Nicole was speechless. *She* was the only secretary in her office. *This can only mean I'm about to be fired*, thought Nicole.

Based upon these perceptions of herself and the surrounding circumstances, Nicole decided to quit. At least she wouldn't lose face. She called her friend Ann, told her that she was quitting, and notified Ann that she was the only applicant for the job.

Ann was hired to take over Nicole's position. On her first day, she looked at the telephone on her desk and noticed the number she'd dialed about the job listing. Ann couldn't believe her eyes. *It wasn't the number from the ad.* She'd dialed the wrong number while job hunting. But she'd been hired anyway!

In a bizarre twist of events, Nicole had just ushered herself out of a job by falling victim to her own self-doubts. But as extreme as her case is, the reasons why it happened are common. Many of us allow apprehensions and insecurities to undermine our confidence. This is an increasingly common condition, as demands on us accelerate and pull us in many different directions at once. (It's increasingly true for men as well, but women especially suffer from these conflicts.)

Our most frightening perceptions often exercise more control over our careers than the truth. Somehow they seem easier to believe than the possibility of potential. As in Nicole's case, perceptions colored by self-doubt create chaos.

Doubting yourself puts self-imposed limitations on you that affect your professional performance. How can clients be confident about what you have to offer, the boss believe you are qualified for a special assignment, or your associates trust your judgment unless you believe in yourself?

If we don't identify what is handicapping our confidence and bridge the gap between our self-image and our true potential, we won't experience the fullness of joy that comes from being God's woman in God's plan. But how do we stop playing mind games and start building our confidence?

BRIDGING THE GAP WITH CONFIDENCE BUILDERS

Bridging the gap between what *is* happening and what we *want* to happen is a challenge. There have been times when I felt like I was building my confidence on quicksand: just about the time I thought I finally had some, it disappeared!

So how *do* we bridge the gap? By taking hold of this truth: *Confidence is a continual choice.* As I mentioned earlier, I'm not just talking about choosing to think positively—because when stress really puts the squeeze on us, it can squeeze out even enough energy to do that. No, I'm talking about *choosing to trust God and reject self-doubt.*

If the key to developing and maintaining confidence lies in trusting God, rather than in how we *feel* about our potential, then we can build a confidence that is rooted deeper than our self-doubt. Instead of flinging a bridge as far across the chasm as our self-image allows us on a given day (which we all know would only rarely make it all the way to the other side), we can step out onto the firm support that God has laid out for us. We can walk across the chasm on the bridge that He has built.

But trusting God is a process, too—not an automatic flip of a switch. There is no generic formula for developing confidence that produces instant results: Trust God and presto!—you surge forth in eager expectation. Instead, the process is like being a scientist in the middle of an experiment that no one else really believes in. Completing the experiment successfully requires trusting in God and believing in our own potential when others doubt us. It means removing self-imposed limitations that stifle our creativity and having faith that the results will reveal a confident woman whom others will believe in.

Sure sounds like a tall order, doesn't it? And it is. But confidence begins simply with a *willingness*—a willingness to believe in our internal capacity and to expect that God will continue to be at work.

This willingness can start with being honest about the condition of our own confidence, and then doing something about it. For example, there are many excellent books out on the market dealing with self-esteem. But there are also some simple basics that we should be doing all the time. Here are a few suggestions for how to build confidence. Use them as leverage to lift the weight of self-doubt and raise your value in the marketplace.

Trust God's Promises over Self-Doubts
Trusting God's promises is our most powerful leverage in moving the dead weight of self-doubt. But often His promises seem hard

to grasp and apply. We try to see ourselves as God sees us — made of "good stuff" — only to have self-doubt keep popping up. Conflicts on the job make us question our abilities. Disappointments grow into justifications for negative thinking — I should have received a raise; I should have gotten that recognition; I should have been chosen over the other person.

In the end, *confidence lies in trusting God unconditionally.* No matter how often we fall short of our expectations, or the marketplace challenges our potential, or others try to make us doubt, trusting God renews our confidence in knowing that even if no one else believes in us, He does.

When we link our trust in God with belief in ourselves, we discover *there is power in believing.* Living in a survivalist mode doesn't make use of that power. God wants us to transform our thinking and believe in the quality of His product — us — and in the quality of His plan: "For I know the plans I have for you . . . plans to prosper you and not to harm you, plans to give you hope and a future."[4]

Those hard days at work take on a new sense of purpose when we choose to trust God's promise that He has a plan for our lives. This trust boosts us into another mode of living, for *believing is the dynamic force that forges our potential into confident actions.* It's a vigorous process that creates higher levels of competency in our performances. I say "vigorous" because it involves not just *saying* we believe, but *taking actions* on our belief. Together, trust and belief unleash our awesome potential and the confidence to use it.

Take an Inventory of Your Personal Resources

There are many tools available today for assessing individual tendencies and characteristics: personal aptitudes, strengths and weaknesses, personality patterns, and so on. Taking inventory of your personal resources — such as natural abilities or emotional strengths and weaknesses — can build confidence in several ways.

First, assessing your resources will tell you where your aptitudes lie. This can help you put your energies to good use wisely and maximize your chances of success. It will also alert you to recognize opportunities that you might otherwise overlook and let slip away.

Kimberly discovered that her analytical mind was not suited to the routines of accounting. However, with additional education and putting her communication skills to use, she became an excellent tax attorney.

Second, an inventory lets you know your areas of weakness. With this knowledge you can take detours in order to avoid wandering into a blind alley. There are some weak areas in which, no matter how hard we work, we will never excel. Admitting this doesn't mean you lack confidence — it means you have common sense.

I love to sing, but I'm tone deaf. My best friend and I were joking one day when she told me, "I'll have no problem finding you if you get to Heaven first: I'll just listen for a 'squawk, squawk' in the heavenly choir!" We laughed, but it wouldn't be funny if I wasted valuable time trying to become a singer while pumping myself up with "I THINK I can." I just don't have the voice.

On the other hand, some weaknesses can be turned into strengths. For example, my mother always told me my mouth would be my ruination, and rightfully so. During one time in my life when I couldn't find the strength in myself I needed, I prayed, "Lord, if you will use my weakness, I will be your witness." It shouldn't have surprised me that after a much-needed refining process, public speaking became my forte.

Set Attainable Goals
Another way to build confidence is through making progress. One of the best ways to do this is to set small goals that you can attain in a short period of time.

As you monitor your progress in achieving these goals, you can learn from your failures and enjoy the benefits of your successes. Both will give you important history on which to base future decisions. The more decision-making skills you develop, the more confident you will become.

We all need to set goals in order to increase our expertise. The sense of being capable gives us momentum to keep stretching ourselves, while our accomplishments reinforce our confidence—"I THOUGHT I could." It was a glorious day when my husband offered to assist a gentleman customer and received the response, "That's okay—I'll just wait for Sheila to be free to help me." The thrill of victory!

I had increased my expertise through working hard and constantly trying to learn. I had learned to believe in myself. My greatest reward was in knowing I had given myself purposefully—and finding out that it had made a difference. Confidence makes a job well done a joy in itself—it doesn't require an audience or a victim.

Pick Your Battles
Don't put yourself into unnecessary positions in which your confidence could be cut down.

Lynn, a customer service manager for an international food company, thrives on accomplishments. She believes one reason her confidence remains strong is that she does not test it in unnecessary confrontations at work. Her associates sometimes ask her, "Why don't you get upset about these office conflicts the way most of us do?" She answers, "I'm confident that I can do the job this company asks of me. That's what counts. Some conflicts aren't worth the commotion: I pick and choose my battles."

Selecting those things you can be effective in doing something about will give meaning to your presence in the marketplace. But allowing yourself to get drawn into unproductive conflicts can drain off your confidence and confuse your perspective. It *creates* chaos.

Project Yourself Confidently
Confidence breeds confidence. You can't control other people, but you can influence how they respond to you by the way you project yourself.

I was working with a woman recently whose competence I doubted. As I analyzed why I doubted her ability, I realized it was because she never looked me in the eyes while she was talking. She looked away from me, as if she didn't want my expressions to question what she was saying. She influenced me the wrong way by indicating that she lacked confidence in herself.

By contrast, one of my most valuable employees sold me on her value because she looked me in the eyes and said, "I think I can do anything that needs to be done." Then she showed me it was true.

How can you project confidence? Eye contact is a good start. Enthusiasm is a good "restarter." I'm not talking about "flying high," but about an energetic outlook that brings others alongside. Enthusiasm is contagious. It's also easily lost in stressful circumstances on the job. In order to be motivating, confidence must have the right foundation. The word *enthusiasm* derives from two Greek words: *en theos*, meaning "in God." True enthusiasm comes from confidence in God. Confidence projected with enthusiasm creates an environment that promotes growth, professional excellence, and long-lasting results.

Express Your Womanhood with Poise

In *My Fair Lady*, Professor Higgins laments, "Why can't a woman be more like a man?" Who wants to? Losing our femininity would rob us of the uniqueness God created us with. One thing we can have confidence in without questioning is that we were created to be God's *woman*. Trying to be one of the guys can lead to self-destructive behavior.

Some women sacrifice who they really are and pay dearly to become who they want to be. Jazz artist Billy Tipton lived under an assumed identity as a male performer. Only after her death was her true identity revealed. In order to seize an opportunity not yet open to women, Billy had hidden her womanhood and spent thirty years as a man.

What a price to pay to receive the applause of the world! What an emptiness when the applause stops. It's self-destructive to deny who we are in order to accomplish a goal, no matter what that goal might be.

What does poised womanhood look like? Let's turn to a portrait of confidence in action.

As a divorced, single parent, Ruth had had her share of circumstances that undermine confidence. But she refused to buy into an anxious frame of mind. She took an inventory of her assets and concluded that she was an enterprising, intelligent woman. She decided to make a disciplined effort to reinforce her ability to make things happen.

Changes didn't happen overnight, but her confidence continually blossomed until its true value paid dividends. One day at work Ruth was forced into the middle of a major crisis with a key client. She found herself confronted by an irate man yelling, "No wonder your company has problems—they send a woman to do a man's job!"

Ruth had three options: retreat, retaliate, or respond. Although she had to work hard at not being intimidated or angered, her confidence prevailed. She chose to respond with her usual caring attitude. Confident of her ability to handle the situation, Ruth remained calm and proposed a resolution to the crisis with her company's client. After a cooling down period and much consideration, the company accepted Ruth's solution *and* offered her a top management position.

How did confidence make a difference for Ruth? First, *she chose to develop confidence in herself.* Second, *she identified her weaknesses and strengths* and increased her capabilities with further training. Third, *she used insights from past decisions* to put together a portfolio of successful strategies for increasing her effectiveness. When she was put on the defensive, *she chose to be a poised woman.* She knew her job could be a man's job, but it wasn't. It was hers, and she took pride in being a competent woman. And last but not least, *she projected herself with confidence*, displayed enthusiasm for her tasks, and maintained a caring attitude.

CONQUERING THE FEAR OF FAILURE

As we move ahead, we need to fight back against the debilitating attacks of fear and self-doubt that will inevitably be there. As

Nicole found out, giving in to these anxieties can result in self-sabotage.

We need to face these doubts head on, knowing that we may fail but remembering that God is in control. When we look at the future this way, we can let go of needing to know how it's all going to turn out. Knowing that we may fail doesn't mean it won't be painful if and when it happens. But it does mean that we don't have to view failure as final. It's just part of the process God is taking us through.

When we quit, we allow fear to rob us of the joy of knowing that at least we gave it our best shot. I have a motto: *I may fail, but I won't quit.*

But even success can trigger fears that rob us of our confidence—not being able to maintain our level of performance; not being accepted by those around us; not being adequate to handle the new responsibilities.

I find it helpful to look at both success and failure through God's viewing lens: the motives of the heart. I believe that when we are seeking to fulfill God's plan, *there is no failure—just stepping stones.* But if we seek to succeed at all costs, there is no success—just stumbling blocks.

God's vantage point keeps us from being whining losers and insufferable winners. It allows us to learn from our disappointments and enjoy our accomplishments, using all of them to build confidence.

OUR CONFIDENCE FLOW

Circumstances in your past may have created chaos in your life. But you don't have to live in the ruins of old experiences. You can *choose* to develop confidence. It's a step-by-step process, revealing what and who you were created to be. It's also an emotional and spiritual process, sweeping away those agonizing doubts and self-defeating feelings and replacing them with a fresh wind of inspiration and strength.

A devotional reading I came across recently speaks of the countless icebergs floating through the frigid waters around

Greenland. Some icebergs are small; others tower skyward. They move in different directions because the tiny ones are affected by wind currents, while the huge, deep ones move only with ocean currents.[5]

Our confidence is subject to two similar forces. When it's based on surface issues it can be controlled by the winds of criticism, competition, and sabotage. But when it reaches down into a deeper power, it's not shaken by the adverse gusts of everyday living. The sure movement of God's purpose and the deep flow of His unchanging love keep us confidently moving with Him—not against the current. The deeper our confidence in God, the more difficult for the crosswinds of the marketplace to affect us.

The Scripture passage that went along with this devotional reading is a well-known description of the Apostle Paul's great trials in carrying out his missionary purpose. My paraphrase of it goes like this: Because of God's love and mercy we have *confidence*—that is, the knowledge of our purpose. It resides in minds that can be adversely affected by external forces and internal thoughts. We have been designed that way to show that our strength comes from the all-surpassing power of God, not from ourselves. "We are hard pressed on every side, but not crushed; perplexed, but not in despair; persecuted, but not abandoned; struck down, but not destroyed."[6] All this is so that our confidence can overflow into the marketplace for God's glory, reaching more and more people.

When the woman of the nineties is sure of where her power comes from, she can cay, "I KNOW I can!" She will experience the strength that comes with confidence. She will feel good about her choices, her work, and herself in the midst of chaos.

It has been a journey for me—sometimes a difficult one—to see myself as God does: with loving realism. At first, my struggle to drive out negative feelings with optimistic "self-talk" only found more ego-deflating thoughts ready to creep in.

But as I have practiced living in the freedom of my purpose, I've found that confidence motivates us when others doubt us, associates discourage us, and friends or family don't understand us. It keeps us going when the world looks lousy and we're not doing so great ourselves. It gives us strength on days when we question if we're brave enough, smart enough, and worth enough to be a good investment.

Let's cling to this bottom line: *When we feel unsure and frightened in the marketplace, we can be confident that God is there — and that He is in us.* With our constancy of purpose as an anchor and the assurance of His presence to empower us, we have the confidence we need to believe the impossible as we develop a vision for the incredible things that can happen in our lives. Our DNA — direction, nature, and actions — frees us to live in expectation of what God is going to do in and through us.

When we move forward in freedom, purpose, and confidence, we stop drifting aimlessly with the current or shifting course every time the wind changes direction. We can't control the winds or the tides of the marketplace, but we can adjust the sails and direct our potential. We can set our sights on the vision that lies ahead.

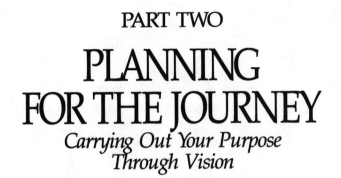

PART TWO

PLANNING FOR THE JOURNEY

Carrying Out Your Purpose
Through Vision

▼▼▼▼▼▼

CHAPTER THREE

SET YOUR SIGHTS WITH ACTION-VISION
▼▼▼▼▼▼
The only limits are, as always, those of vision.[1]

My heart started pounding harder and harder the closer I got to the door of our local bank. I had the entrepreneurial jitters.

I was excited about our new business venture. Now one of our first moments of truth was upon us. When Bob, the vice president, asked for our business plan, projections, and financial statements, I was prepared. As we discussed the business I talked about John's archery expertise, innate salesmanship, and natural mechanical abilities. Bob looked at me quizzically and said, "But Sheila — I thought the plan was for you to run the business. What can you do?"

For the first time, I was being asked about my capabilities other than those connected to being John's wife or the mother of Terri and John. I was going to have to make it on my own in this big, fast, unforgiving business world.

I looked Bob straight in the eye and said, "I've got my smile." Of all the replies Bob's ever received, I'm sure that one had to be the most brazen.

I answered that way because Bob had caught me off-guard. He had gotten personal. I had been focusing on a vision for the *business,* not for *me.* Oh, sure — I could explain to Bob what I would be doing in the new venture, but I had not seen the assets I would be bringing to it as clearly as I had seen John's. I didn't yet have the bigger picture of who I was and how my new position fit into that portrait.

Now that I have not only developed a vision but experienced how visions can become reality, I look back on that day at the bank and realize how naive I really was. Not about my role in the business, but about my lack of vision for merging my career, my family, and my personal needs.

I understood my purpose. I had my priorities in order. But like so many women who go to work, I took on a career without making adjustments to my household or personal commitments. I got into a routine of overextending my days. I wasn't just working overtime; I was working all the time just trying to keep up with my work. I found I was *doing things right*, but not *doing the right things*.

Let me explain. I was working efficiently to complete all my tasks—putting in overtime to meet deadlines, staying up late to finish the laundry, buying the first outfit I tried on just to be dressed properly for a special event. In other words, I was reacting to circumstances, always doing the next thing that had to be done.

But I wasn't doing the *right* things—saying no to excess demands in order to meet a deadline, delegating responsibilities for home maintenance, taking a few hours out for myself to replace my deteriorating wardrobe.

I needed to be doing what was important, not just what was putting pressure on me.

VISION: BLUEPRINT FOR ACHIEVEMENT

My early experiences in running a business (while being a wife, mother, person, and so on) taught me that doing things right is *efficient*, but not necessarily *effective*.

Why is it so important to do the *right* things? To understand, I went back to business principles. There I was reminded how vital it is to have a sense of direction. If you don't plan for how and why you want a business to grow, you won't have any sound basis for making decisions—whether day by day or long range.

Just as our new venture had to have a business plan—a vision of what we wanted the business to become and how we planned to get there, too—so I needed a vision for why and how I was going to make a contribution to the marketplace. This vision needed to be big enough to fit my whole life in it—my family, my personal needs, the future of my career—not just what my responsibilities would be at the Archery Center.

In order to develop a clear understanding of what gives meaning to our efforts, we need *vision*. Vision builds on purpose as a key ingredient for moving beyond chaos and taking charge of our careers. In order to direct our lives instead of drifting, we need a clear understanding of what we want to achieve.

The term *vision* has been used as a lofty way of referring to many things—long-range plans, hopes, dreams, even wishful thinking. Therefore, it's important to clarify how I'll be using this term. Basically, when I use the term *vision* I'm referring to *a picture of desired results*. It's an image of what we want to happen.

Vision is dynamic, not static. As my life changes, my vision refocuses accordingly, but I always have in front of me an image of what I want to become and accomplish. Purpose is my reason for being, but vision is the outcome of the methods I choose to fulfill my purpose. Vision gives purpose somewhere to go. It's the compass that keeps us going in the right direction; the blueprint with which we build tomorrow, today.

In his book *Thriving on Chaos*, Tom Peters describes effective visions as "beacons and controls when all else is up for grabs."[2] For me, vision is the spotlighted target that keeps me focused when everything seems out of control.

For example, consider a secretary who pictures herself as a sales associate rather than viewing her position as a dead-end street. Or a licensed practical nurse who, frustrated with the limitations of her involvement in patients' care, works to become a registered nurse. Or a company president who targets a better work environment for her employees rather than giving up on the situation. These desired results serve as signposts to remind them of what they're working toward. They are pictures of what they are committed to achieving.

But it takes more than hopes and dreams to build a vision—it takes a focused life. Sadly, many of us live out our lives without ever connecting our daily reality to the hopes and dreams we've cherished within.

When I've polled women in my seminars on their needs, they give me a list. When I ask about their dreams, they pull out their entire "hope chest." When I ask for their vision, however, they draw a blank. This is not surprising—because most of us are not aware of what vision is and why it's so important.

Most of us think of dreams, needs, and visions as the same thing. They're not. Think for a moment about needs and dreams. A need is something essential that's waiting to be met. A dream is effortless—something we wake up from or simply hope for, something we wish would happen. We all have needs and dreams. And we all need a vision, which takes those needs and dreams one step further: *vision gives us hope that our needs can be met and inspires us to make our dreams become reality.*

This power of vision to fulfill needs and turn dreams into reality is what I call *action-vision*. Action-vision is *an image of desired results that inspires us to action.* It's more than just a snapshot from our hope chest. It's a visualization of the *possibilities,* the *probabilities,* and the *process* of making things happen.

Action-vision doesn't mean developing a tunnel vision of what we think our life should be like and then feeling we've missed the mark when it doesn't happen. Instead, it's recognizing the desires of our heart and being actively involved in the process of seeing them become reality or being willing to revamp the blueprints. In this mode of living, God's will is not some elusive dream, but a daily reality. It's a method of setting direction for the future that allows us to live fully today.

Let's take a look at how this remarkable concept operates. To live in an action-vision mode, here are the characteristics we need to be fine-tuning:

1. *Our thinking is positive and forward-looking.* Because we're motivated to turn our vision into reality, we're on the lookout for

opportunities. When we're confronted with the changing circumstances of a turbulent business environment, our vision gives us a reference point for making adjustments in order to stay prepared for what's coming. It will also keep us from making choices that move us in the wrong direction.

Forward thinking enables us to see dead-end streets, such as stenographers met when computers and tape recorders limited the need for shorthand. Taking action to develop new skills to keep up with changing technology kept them in a progressive field in the marketplace.

Thinking positively also focuses our attention on future potential and helps keep us from feeling sapped by the "empty vision" syndrome when one stage of life is transitioning to another.

2. *We are willing to accept responsibility for taking action.* We know that to meet the challenges of the marketplace, we must take a proactive instead of a reactive approach. We're realistic about what it's going to take to make things happen.

3. *We know how to make choices.* Because we adjust our visions as we see how pieces fit together to offer new opportunities or close doors, life proceeds on a more realistic basis, rather than on wishful thinking. We learn how to make wise choices.

We're also motivated to make choices as our vision ignites our passion of purpose, channeling and directing our drive to persevere toward desired results.

4. *We anticipate accomplishment.* Action-vision is ignited by our passion of purpose. It then channels and directs that drive toward our desired results as we anticipate accomplishment.

Golfer Jack Nicklaus describes how he envisions what he wants to happen as well as how he will make it happen when he anticipates accomplishment in his sport:

> I never hit a shot, even in practice, without having a very sharp, in-focus picture of it in my head. First I "see" the ball where I want it to finish, nice and white and sitting up high on the bright green grass. Then the scene quickly changes and I "see" the ball going there: its path, trajectory, and shape, even its behavior on landing. Then there's

a sort of fade-out, and the next scene shows me making the kind of swing that will turn the previous images into reality.[3]

The practice of visualization has taken a bad rap in some circles because of its appropriation by so-called New Age movements. As I use it, however, it's a healthy practice of insights and implementation. Chuck Swindoll puts it beautifully when he says:

> Vision is the ability to see above and beyond the majority. Vision is perception—reading the presence and power of God into one's circumstances. I sometimes think of vision as looking at life through the lens of God's eyes, seeing situations as He sees them. Too often we see things not as they are, but as we are.[4]

This crucial habit of seeing things through God's eyes, and developing a vision of what we're in process toward, gives us the sense that God is our partner in daily decisions. It makes the difference between floating through life with a let-it-happen attitude and acting on the realization that life's too precious not to make the most of it.

MAKING IT HAPPEN

Action-vision never just happens. It is a creative, ongoing process. Like Jack Nicklaus watching himself make the perfect golf swing, we must play a continual mental videotape of what we want to happen. We should be visualizing the path we'll be following, the pace of our progress, and how we're going to behave as we move forward.

Here are some insights for developing your own action-vision:

1. *Make sure that your vision represents your true objectives.* Your image of desired results should be a picture of what you want to be doing with your life. Your vision will continue to reflect this desire if you keep track of changing needs and circumstances and adjust your vision accordingly.

As an example, consider Jane, who found herself frustrated with an unfulfilled vision to own her own company in order to do advanced research in marine biology. She couldn't picture any other way to achieve her objectives. However, when her employer unexpectedly promoted her she was enabled to fulfill her vision for marine science without assuming the liabilities of becoming a business owner.

Until her circumstances opened up her vision for how to act on her dreams, Jane had been stuck in the assumption that there was only one way to meet her goal. Action-vision should reflect *what we want to accomplish, not the position we want to hold.* Jane's vision was research, not entrepreneurship.

2. *Make a visual blueprint of the territory you'll be covering to achieve your goals.* Staking out your territory will keep you focused on creating the desired results. Territory means the areas you're responsible for — family, community commitments, professional demands, and so on. This doesn't mean you're fencing yourself in, but rather that you're establishing reasonable guidelines to keep from overextending yourself. Knowing your territory will help you respond wisely rather than impulsively to opportunities.

3. *Develop the underlying fundamentals that build the characteristics of a discerning heart, an understanding mind, and the power of commitment.* These foundations of action-vision are the key to moving ahead effectively, communicating clearly, and staying committed to a focused effort.

A Discerning Heart
This character trait is based on the truth that *what a woman thinks in her heart will determine who she becomes and how her vision takes shape.*

Vision is the instrument with which we direct our lives. A discerning heart keeps that instrument tuned so we can use it effectively. It gives us the ability to grasp whether or not the options, motives, and methods that lie between us and our vision are dangers or opportunities.

With discernment, we can tell creative ideas from figments

of our imagination. If we dream of becoming the first woman president of the United States, discernment will let us know whether to keep dreaming or start politicking.

A discerning heart keeps us in tune with others. It is in the heart that our vision has an unending capacity to reach out and connect with others, meeting their needs. But at the same time, our heart tells us when we're doing too much. Discernment is what keeps our life within appropriate limitations.

Read the book of Proverbs and you'll get a wealth of lessons on a discerning heart. Proverbs tells us that discerning individuals learn quickly, speak with wisdom, stand out in a crowd, focus on what's important, stay on track in pursuit of their goals, and learn from their mistakes.[5]

How do we develop a discerning heart? The best place to start is by *spending time with God*. Through prayer, Bible reading, and fellowship with others who are also seeking divine guidance for their lives, we become sensitive to His principles. As we apply these principles in the marketplace, we exercise discernment.

For example, the Apostle Paul instructs us to be "not slothful in business; fervent in spirit; serving the Lord."[6] When questions of business ethics come up, this passage can help us discern the proper course of action—such as working with integrity rather than taking shortcuts.

Another way to develop discernment is to *become a real listener*. This means hearing what others are really saying—and to do this we must develop in-depth listening skills. Listening is becoming a lost art—and this loss accounts for many missed opportunities.

Marie's listening skills opened up her big career break. As she listened to her boss discussing his work overload, she heard his unspoken cry for help. Marie suggested some solutions, which ultimately led to a major promotion.

It wasn't just a desire for advancement that made Marie a discerning person. Her ability to identify needs developed from listening, evaluating, and then recommending. When we listen to others we not only learn new things, we gain more insight with which to make assessments.

Women with action-vision value a discerning heart as crucial to making their mark in the marketplace. Although earning money and receiving occasional recognitions are rewarding, they are not the ultimate payback. Real joy comes from being able to discern needs in a way that enables a woman of vision to influence others to take hold of her vision or develop their own.

Marsha provides a good example of this influence. She had an employee who was spending so much time feeling sorry for herself over her unhappy personal situation that she wasn't getting her work done. Marsha could see that Tanya would be a valuable asset to the company if she applied herself. So Marsha decided she would take Tanya to lunch and talk to her about her work situation.

During lunch, Marsha asked Tanya, "If you tried on a beautiful dress that fit perfectly but was overpriced, would you buy it anyway?"

Tanya admitted she wouldn't.

"That's what is happening with you," Marsha went on. "I thought you were perfect for the job, but I can't afford you for what I'm getting. You'll be a great asset if you give me what you've got to give. Let's work together."

Today, Tanya is Marsha's right hand. Tanya uses the same type of discernment that Marsha modeled to develop action-visions for herself and to supervise her employees. This turnaround occurred because Marsha's discerning heart enabled her to see potential. Marsha listened to her employee's personal needs and took steps to create opportunity out of chaos.

An Understanding Mind

A second fundamental character trait essential to developing action-vision is *an understanding mind*. This is crucial for thinking creatively and making wise decisions.

A common behavior pattern that many of us fall into is withdrawing from a particular situation because we are preoccupied with immediate obstacles instead of focusing on a constructive solution. Our mind rationalizes, "I'd do it *except.* . . ." An understanding mind can help us take charge instead of give up.

If you find yourself in this kind of approach-avoidance circumstance, tackle the *excepts*. Don't just bypass them and settle for conventional assumptions. Instead, look ahead at where
your vision is taking you, and draw your own conclusions about
which routes to take.

That's just what Cheryl did. Cheryl loved to see people
smile when they heard a beautiful song. She thought to herself, "I would love to touch people with music . . . *except* I can't
sing." In this situation, some people might write off their desire
as wishful thinking. But Cheryl's vision impelled her to take
action. She learned how to read and compose music, and then
she started writing ballads. She bypassed the *excepts* and fulfilled
her vision.

What enabled Cheryl to override her limitations and develop
her possibilities? She understood her lack of musical potential as
a singer. She understood the alternatives. And she understood
what actions she had to take to make her vision for music become
reality.

Understanding makes possible the wisdom to recognize
limitations as well as the courage to find other ways. It gives
us knowledge of ourselves: "The purposes of a man's heart are
deep waters, but a man of understanding draws them out," says
the writer of Proverbs.[7]

How do we develop an understanding mind? Consider these
statements from the Bible:

◆ "The fear of the LORD is the beginning of wisdom; all
  who follow his precepts have good understanding."[8]
◆ "Trust in the LORD with all your heart and lean not on
  your own understanding; in all your ways acknowledge
  him, and he will make your paths straight."[9]
◆ "A patient man has great understanding, but a quick-
  tempered man displays folly."[10]

Understanding grows as we patiently work through obstacles and learn from experience. However, God offers us the gift
of understanding and makes His wisdom available to us as we

seek His guidance for the challenges, opportunities, and stresses of our lives.

The Power of Commitment

Vision without action is dead. If we don't go for it, it's never going to happen.

To make a commitment means *to be an active participant*. It means turning something theoretical into something actual. It's powerful.

Putting the power of commitment to work in our vision involves allocating our resources for earnest striving to pursue our purpose. This is what brings our vision into the here-and-now instead of the out-of-touch. It's how we stay involved in what's happening around us, using feedback to influence our choices and keep us growing. The uniqueness of our individual presence enables us to be confident in who we are and what we can become.

To paraphrase the Apostle Paul, "I'm not where I want to be yet. But I'll keep pressing on in the here-and-now. I won't keep tripping over the stumbling blocks of the past, but use them as stepping stones as I keep growing. I will stretch my potential to make my vision — what I want to accomplish — become a reality."[11]

In other words, I'll take the challenge as the new computer programmer, knowing it will open other doors of opportunity. I'll remember the big blunder I made in the last audit only to help me be more accurate in the future. I'll work on my master's degree so I can move into educational administration. I'll deepen my commitment to personal growth by developing daily visions based on Scripture that I can apply at work.

HOW TO SHARPEN YOUR VISION

Turning our visions into reality in an accelerating marketplace is a challenge. To paraphrase Shakespeare, all the world's a stage, and we're all understudies continually being cast in new roles.

This climate of change is why the issue of vision is crucial and cries for attention from all levels of society. Action-vision enables us to move with the current of change instead of struggling against it.

A particular need of the working woman is to coordinate all the varying agendas of her life so they are in harmony with each other. Otherwise, she will be pulled in as many different directions as she has agendas.

Therefore, *developing a vision that merges all the agendas of our lives is essential to being effective in the marketplace.* Without this integrating vision, the fragmentation will tear us into bits and pieces.

The purpose of this chapter has been to help you grasp how important it is to be a personal visionary, to see that there is a purpose beyond chaos. Although women working is nothing new, ours is the first generation of women who not only have been given the option of a personal vision but who suffer the consequences of not having one. Action-vision helps us to find creative solutions to chaotic conditions.

Recently I spoke with a CEO of a multi-million-dollar company. She had a vision—a very successful one, I might add. But it was only for her business. She commented, "I feel like I'm missing 'it,' but I don't know what 'it' is."

As we talked, I discovered that our CEO had lost any vision of developing a personal life. She felt "it" had passed her by.

But it's never too late to recover lost visions or develop new ones. I told this lonely executive the story of the lady who lost all hope for the future when her husband died. In her bleak despair, she had his tombstone inscribed with "The light has gone out in my life."

Several years later the widow shared with a friend her guilt over what she had placed on her husband's tombstone, because now she had a new vision and a new life. "What can I do?" she asked her friend.

"Add this line to his epitaph," her friend wisely replied: "'So I struck another match.'"

What the "it" is that's missing depends upon the individual—it could be the development of a personal talent, a lasting relationship, or a consistent career path. None of us can afford to put our decision-making process on autopilot. We need to customize our own vision by merging our agendas according to what is best for our particular set of circumstances. The benefits, and the consequences, of those choices are long-term.

There are widows and divorced women in the marketplace who do not have a vision for the future—they're just trying to survive *today*. There are college students who prepare for the future only to confront the workplace confused about how to use their education. There are women returning to work after long stretches out of the marketplace who think age and past skills are blockades. Lacking vision, women in these circumstances drift where others think they should go.

Then there are times when we *do* have an idea of what we want, but we have no idea how to get there. Or as hard as we try, we just can't seem to make it happen. What then?

KEEP YOUR VISION IN SIGHT

I once saw a comic strip that showed a little girl drawing a picture. "Who are you drawing?" her mother asked.

"God," responded the little girl.

"But honey," her mother quickly reminded her, "you can't draw God. Nobody knows what He looks like."

The little girl sat up straight, looked directly at her mother, and said very confidently, "They will when *I* get through."

When I read this it was like someone had just turned on the light. I realized, *Purpose gives me the understanding and confidence I need to develop my own vision of what being God's woman in God's plan looks like—for me.* What a realization! At that point, no one—not even I—knew yet what that plan for fulfilling my purpose in the marketplace would look like. But *God* knew, and He had written the outline. Now I would be filling in the details of individualized abilities and God-given desires to customize my specific agendas.

This realization simultaneously calmed and excited me. I had my "reason for being," my freedom to be in it, and the knowledge that the way to accomplish it was through a vision of what and who I wanted to become. I began to piece together the elements of action-vision: inherent talent, past experience, insights based on discernment and understanding, and implementation in the here-and-now.

Our dreams may differ, but we all share the same desires for accomplishment, acceptance, and love. Our individuality shows in the particular ways we see to fulfill these desires. A secretary sees a management opportunity; a nurse sees an intimate way to touch hurting lives; a vice president sees how to be a mentor; a teacher sees how to develop young minds.

Visions arise out of the needs and concerns of individual human beings like you and me. Each of us has the legitimate right to pursue the visions that God has put within us. Be sure you don't compromise *your* vision. Don't settle for being a corporate manager if your vision is to be a physical therapist. Don't resign yourself to "just a job" when your heart is yearning for a deeper commitment.

In the next several chapters, I'll be exploring with you how to develop your own action-visions — for personal growth, for relationships, for career. You'll learn how to sketch a picture of your own customized plan — and then we'll go on in part 3 to the process of implementing your visions a step at a time. I want you to begin experiencing the relief of purposeful living by the time you finish this book.

I have written this book because of a vision. I see chaos in the lives of working women. But I have a vision of joy beyond chaos in the midst of a stress-filled marketplace.

What has enabled me to pursue the vision of empowering women in the marketplace has been *discernment* — to recognize the pain of trying to overcome my past failures, the fears of pioneering new territory, and the motives behind my attempts to become superwoman. It took *understanding* of the needs — my own and those of working women — that I recognized through my experiences. Acting on my vision also required that I apply *the power of commitment* to persevere.

Developing a vision that merges our agendas is a tremendously beneficial investment for our journey through the market-place. We will look forward, not backward. We won't mind so much digging deep into our resources because we will know why we're doing it and how much we need. Our days will be challenging, but they will also be purposeful. Dreams will no longer be just wishful thinking; they will become blueprints for our ultimate achievements.

CHAPTER FOUR

TAKE CARE OF YOURSELF
▼▼▼▼▼

*The golden opportunity you are seeking is
in yourself. It is not in your environment;
it is not in luck or chance, or the help
of others: it is in yourself alone.*[1]

I looked at Geri and said to her with a big smile, "Yes—it *was*
worth it!"

Geri knew exactly what I meant. We'd both worked so hard
to get out of the office for a few days that we had questioned
whether the trip was worth the effort.

But here we were walking along the beach at Siesta Key, the
hot sun penetrating our tense muscles, the soft sand caressing
our achy feet, and the rolling waves pounding out a soothing
background rhythm in our minds. We knew it was worth it.

I actually began to feel guilty that I was enjoying myself so
much. It was great to be away from it all—the incessant ringing
of the telephone, the endless problem solving, the constant routine of office work, even family responsibilities. These were all
part of a daily life that I cherished, but my problem was that my
daily life couldn't fit into each day anymore. I needed a break to
regroup.

This trip had been a nice surprise. John had noticed how
badly I needed time out and arranged with Geri to give me an
escape vacation for my birthday. For the first time since we had
bought the business, I stepped out of the rat race.

I walked the beach, sat and read a good book — without inter- ruptions! — and even went to bed at eight o'clock. As I began to unwind, I reflected on my personal and professional needs and responsibilities. I needed discernment to know when enough was enough. I needed a vision of how to give *of* myself without giving *up* myself.

Our intricate physical, emotional, and spiritual makeup isn't designed for constant overdrive. But most of us never take the time to put our feet up and call it a day. We find ourselves in a catch-22 situation: *If I don't take time for me, the pressure creates chaos. If I do take time for me, the guilt takes a toll.*

This kind of guilt attacks us on two fronts. First, we feel so guilty about taking personal time that we can't enjoy it or benefit from it. Second, pressure from others makes us feel so guilty that we wish we'd never slowed down. However, using guilt as an excuse not to take care of ourselves is a cop-out.

I can hear some of you protesting already: "Now just wait a minute! You don't know all the demands on me — caring for my elderly parents, a boss who expects continual overtime, a family who assumes I should be superwoman. I'm already out of time, and now you want me to do something *else.*"

But I'm not questioning your workload. I'm questioning *how long you will be able to maintain it.*

Today's working woman is way overextended. Today, more than ever, you need to know when enough is too much. You need to believe that *it's all right to take care of yourself.*

As I strolled the beach and gazed at the waves lapping against the shore, I began to think about how much difference this time of recreation meant to me. For the first time, I began to see recreation as *re-creation.*

TAKING TIME FOR YOU

Re-creation is a renewing and restoring of self — a refreshment of strength and spirit. I'm using this term because I want to empha- size that personal time can provide more than just a change of scenery or a period of relaxation. In a deeper sense, it can be a period of rebuilding. It not only relieves stress; it injects strength.

Taking time to renew yourself will give your action-vision new gusto for making your marketplace adventures and personal relationships vibrant. Re-creation is essential for personal growth and professional excellence. It will increase your enthusiasm, energy, and efficiency. If you want to live beyond chaos instead of as a victim of chaos, re-creation is not an option, it is a must.

Have you heard the story of the two woodcutters? One of them kept cutting all day long, stopping only long enough to eat lunch. The other stopped cutting every hour for a few minutes' break.

The first woodcutter, seeing that the second had chopped far more wood than he, exclaimed in disbelief, "I don't understand why you have double the wood that I do! You took so many breaks, while I took none!"

The second woodcutter answered him, "Yes—but while I rested, I sharpened my ax."

We all need to take time to sharpen our tools. But personal time doesn't have to be a vacation get-away. We can take it in bite-sized pieces: a few minutes to sit on a park bench, a brief interlude to read a short article, an extra cup of coffee to pause and reflect before starting the day. But these little bites must be part of a steady diet of consistent time set aside for you—for revitalizing your physical strength, renewing your spirit, regrouping your thoughts.

Today's working woman is not, however, making choices to take care of herself. She isn't really convinced that creating her own time is a legitimate ambition. Oh, sure, it's acceptable to take time for business meetings, school shopping for the children, even lunch with a friend. But how many of us would be horrified if someone found out we excused ourselves from an invitation because our *own* time was more important?

Stop right now and ask yourself, "Am I too busy to set aside time for *me*?" If you answered yes, then you are the very woman I'm addressing.

Get out your calendar. Schedule in time for yourself. In that space, write "O-W-N." It means:

Not that I *Ought* to because I should or
Not that I *Want* to because it's fun (even though that's
    valid too)
But that I *Need* to because it helps shape me into the
    person I envision becoming.

Get in the habit of thinking "O-W-N." Say to yourself regularly, "I'm taking this time for me not just because I ought to or want to, but because I *need* to." Envision the results of taking care of yourself — better health, more energy and enjoyment, increased mental and emotional clarity, a deeper spiritual dimension in your life. Once you've worked through the O-W-N process in your mind, your choices will begin to change.

A QUIET PLACE FOR YOUR SPIRIT

The idea of a quiet place is a lost concept in our high-tech world. Even the most remote islands are within the sound of jets overhead.

But we all need moments apart from the noisy clamor of our worlds. We need somewhere we can go — a park, a patio, behind a closed door — and know that this is our O-W-N quiet place.

A quiet place is the setting for taking care of our spirit. It's the meeting place where we get in touch with ourselves and with God. "Be still and know that I am God," quotes the psalmist.[2] We need this stillness in order to become aware of God's presence in our lives. Here in the quiet, we become sensitive to what God wants to do through us. We can envision what He has planned. We can tell Him our desires and our struggles. We can delight in Him.

When we neglect our need to be alone and quiet before God it will eventually produce loneliness, emptiness, and disappointment. Why? Because we lose touch with our dreams and visions. When this happens, we often lose touch with God's purpose and plan.

In the marketplace, when you're out of cash flow you're out of business. Money truly keeps the working world turning. In the

Christian life, it is the Christ-flow that keeps us moving. We impoverish our spirit without this foundational current of vitality.

Jesus demonstrated the supreme importance of a quiet place for the spirit. He knew what it was like to live in a world full of demands and stress. He had inexperienced people to train. His qualifications were tested at every turn. The chaos of His environment was exhausting. Yet He frequently retreated from the demands of others to be alone and pray. He changed gears without guilt and without losing His sense of direction.

During His greatest trial, when He was facing His appointment at the cross, Jesus spent time in a quiet place in the Garden of Gethsemane. He anguished over the struggle and then collected Himself to respond instead of just react. His time apart enabled Him to maintain His perspective on His purpose for coming. The immediate crisis could not detour Him from His chosen path.

It's not easy to pull back and be still, especially when our minds are busy solving problems and resolving conflicts while the pressure builds. It takes discipline to schedule our own time when the crowds are pushing and pulling on us. But the reward is a healthy spirit and a renewed outlook on life.

Remind yourself to draw the line when enough is too much. When it's time to retreat to a quiet place, don't put it off. Accept the invitation to spend time in the Lord's presence. Make room for *you* in your schedule.

RX FOR YOUR BODY

I received quite a shock the day my doctor told me, "Your reports came back with the typical executive profile." *Oh no*, I thought. *Not me! I don't fit that picture – that's for older, workaholic men. I'm young. I can go nonstop.*

However, the doctor's profile referred not to a person, but to a problem: the consequences of stress. Stress takes a toll on overworked bodies. In my case there was reason for concern. I knew I was pushing myself beyond my limits. I finally had to admit the effects of my Type-A personality, heredity, and not taking care of myself.

My condition could really have been summed up in one word: *exhaustion*. Fatigue saturated my whole being. I was afraid to keep going at such a hectic pace, but I was afraid of what would happen if I slowed down.

During my vacation at the beach I began to understand the true benefits of rest. The rest wasn't just the result of extra sleep or quiet time to myself. It was also relief from stress in friendly chats, long walks, and leisurely exercises. I experienced rest as I took care of *me*.

But as that vacation came to an end I thought, *Well, that was great while it lasted, but what now? In a few days this is going to be just a refreshing memory.* That was true, unless I did something to take care of myself in my own environment.

One change I made was to develop a walking schedule. This works for me. It's something I can continue to do as long as I'm mobile. My husband really puts the pressure on me to stick to it. And even though (in true wifely fashion) I hate to admit he's right, the time I spend relieving stress and exercising for fitness pays big dividends.

I've learned that if I want big dividends from daily self-care, I need to be willing to make a few concessions. Believe it or not, I discovered that the world still goes on just fine if I don't stay up for the eleven o'clock news, and that I'm more rested with seven hours' sleep. I also pay more attention to Sundays, which God in His infinite wisdom set apart as interludes for rest and reflection. After the refreshment of church, time for family, friends, and a good snooze help renew me for the coming week.

Other changes I've made include: taking leisurely baths instead of quick showers . . . turning chores into opportunities, such as wrapping Christmas presents with friends . . . reading a book to shift my mental speed from intense thinking to interesting diversion . . . using my lunch hour to unwind and redirect my day instead of grabbing a quick sandwich at my desk. . . . It seems that simple things help simplify my life, and they give me moments beyond the chaos, even in the midst of it. Have I arrived? No, I still find myself overdoing and under stress. But it doesn't take me as long to return to moments of re-creation.

Taking care of our physical health involves more than just changing behavioral patterns, however. Re-creation also involves changing our thought patterns. In some areas of life, for example, we need to quit being serious and just have fun. Individual or team sports, games with friends, kickball with the kids, a workout at the club—these are all activities that refresh us physically and mentally. It's surprising how easily we can incorporate them into our days when we decide they're valuable.

JOURNALING—YOUR EMOTIONAL MASSAGE

Pam sat across from me, fighting back the tears. "I feel so emotionally drained," she said. "Inside I'm screaming, *Someone take care of me!* Outside I push everyone away. It's during these times that I get so critical of myself and others. And then while I'm looking at what I need to do to keep my insides from turning inside out, I trip over another crisis at the office. It seems like there's no one to talk to."

Like it or not, we all struggle with our emotions. The days when they threaten to overwhelm us can make it unbearable to be at work.

But sadly enough, we don't pay much attention to our emotions except in those cases when they *force* our attention. When we get the flu, we do what's necessary to get better. But when our emotions are suffering, we often neglect them.

Dealing with emotions is a very big subject area. I want to focus on one simple discipline that can help us maintain emotional equilibrium in the marketplace: journaling.

I've kept a journal for many years, carrying it over into my career. Keeping a record of my personal and professional odyssey has been an important tool in my growth and development. It has inspired me by revealing my personal progress. It has moved me to gratitude as I've reflected on the blessings of my life. It has helped me address inner turmoil and work through conflicts. It has given me a place to go with frustrations and disappointments when I felt I could not share them with others.

Sounds like I write epistles, doesn't it? No way! Journaling is my debriefing time. I use it as a relaxing, bite-sized piece of my day in which I recap what is happening in and around me. It's a place where I can reflect in private — kind of like stopping at a red light in the middle of rush-hour traffic. I can relax, take a deep breath, and gather my thoughts.

Sometimes journaling can provide us with the extra room we need to work through challenges *away* from the office instead of *in* the office. Jackie, a capable young attorney, was having difficulty voicing her opinion about office reorganization to her male colleagues. Since they were all adept at arguing cases, they often out-talked her before she had a chance to explain her thoughts. Her frustration level was rising, and so was her temper. She took her struggle to her journal.

Looking back, Jackie later reflected, "Journaling sure helped my career. If I had gone to work and blasted the other attorneys with what was on my mind they would have had enough to hang me," she chuckled. "By journaling my days, I began to organize the chaos. I relieved my frustrations so I could sort out my true thoughts. I ended up carefully presenting my case for how the office should be run, and I won."

I make a point of journaling as positively as I can. Everything that I can write down in a positive mode, without compromising the facts, I do. This has disciplined me to see the positive when I start looking at the negative.

Journaling also helps me stay aware of my visions. I write them down as I identify them, and then I journal about them while they're in progress. I also keep a section of spiritual reflections, in which I write down prayer requests and answers, thoughts about what God is doing in my life, and reflections from Bible reading. All of this keeps me in touch with the deeper currents in my life.

Another benefit I've discovered is that my journal helps keep me honest with myself. It's easier to color the truth when I'm talking or just thinking to myself. Writing something down forces me to tell it like it is.

Several years ago, I added what I call an "Aimpoints" section to my journal. This is where I get down to the nitty-gritty by trying to find the points in me that trigger negative reactions.

I began this practice when the stress of my venture in the marketplace started worsening steadily. I found there were days of emotional turbulence when I felt like a bomb ready to explode, although I wasn't sure why. Writing down my thoughts in a quiet place helped me come to grips with circumstances that were igniting my emotions—especially when I was being demanding of others or when they seemed overly demanding of me.

As I see stressful patterns develop and recognize their source, I take these things to the Lord. It helps me to focus on changing what I can and letting go of what I can't.

Laura found herself constantly becoming angry with different individuals at work. I recommended that she keep a journal with an Aimpoints section. As she started writing down her feelings during these "fits" of anger, she began to realize why they occurred. She was using her anger to put others on the defensive because she was unsure of her own professional abilities.

Equipped with this new insight, Laura stopped and asked herself, "Is this a defense mechanism?" every time her anger began to boil. As she gained control of her temper she found herself advancing through the company. She later learned that her angry disposition had been holding her back.

Journaling has made a difference in me. It has enabled me to see the joys and frustrations of the marketplace in a very honest and private manner. These moments of my days have been well spent. Now I call journaling *my emotional massage.*

To help you take care of your emotional life, make a commitment to try journaling if you're not already doing it. You'll find it rewarding. And don't panic if you miss a few days now and then. In journaling, you don't have to answer to anyone.

Here's my 1-2-3 of journaling: (1) Debrief yourself in twenty to thirty lines. (Feel free to write more or less if you want to; there's no right or wrong way.) I break my thoughts into "me," my relationships, and marketplace happenings. (2) During devotional reflections, write a few lines about how you think God is guiding you or where you seem to be on your spiritual pilgrimage. (3) Whenever stress builds up, write an Aimpoint, reflecting on what the sources are and what you can do about them. And overall, enjoy your journaling as a time of re-creation.

MAINTAINING A MASTERPIECE

Henry David Thoreau wrote in his famous *Walden*, "Our life is frittered away by detail. . . . Simplify! Simplify!"

How often our lives are frittered away by detail. But it doesn't have to be that way. Taking the time to care for yourself isn't easy — but it's not as complicated as you might think.

One way to simplify your agenda for personal care is to take a half day alone to reflect on taking care of "me." Go to a quiet place. Get in touch with your feelings: emotional, physical, spiritual. Think about the blessings you can thank God for. Spend the time discovering what you need for re-creation and how you can incorporate it into your life.

God created each of us as an individual masterpiece. But our responsibility is to maintain this masterpiece. Our vision for becoming a woman of purpose means keeping soul, body, mind, and emotions in sync. We need a process to free ourselves from the debilitating stress of pressures and demands. Even a rubber band snaps when stretched too far. Re-creation gives the joy and strength to follow our God-given path through the marketplace.

Develop an action-vision for maintaining your masterpiece by envisioning how you want to develop personally. What do you want to characterize your life? Peace of mind, physical stamina, a more relaxed demeanor, a joy in sensing God's presence? Envision how these improvements will make your experience in the marketplace less chaotic, how relationships will become more meaningful. Write down the possibilities, probabilities, and processes that are involved in acting on your vision.

As you set your sights on taking care of yourself, you'll be better equipped to understand how to cut through the chaos and make room for personal growth in your working life. And you'll be a lot closer to becoming the kind of person God created you to be.

CHAPTER FIVE

NURTURE YOUR RELATIONSHIPS

We make a living by what we get,
but we make a life by what we give.

I couldn't believe it—the weekend was already here. The hectic week at work had caught up with me, and I was exhausted. I was aching to take a hot bath, settle into a cozy chair with a good book, and vegetate.

I would have no such luck, however. We had company coming for the weekend. My only consolation was that the house would be clean when I got home—I'd carefully arranged that with my family.

When I walked through the front door, the smile on my lips vanished as I dropped my jaw, stunned at what I was seeing. The house was in a state of chaos. My son was waiting for a ride to ball practice, and the television held everyone captive.

I dropped into the nearest chair and began surveying the bedlam. I threw visual daggers at anyone within eye range. Then I let them have it with both barrels: "Can't you do *anything* I ask? I don't ask much. It would be nice for me, too, if I had a mom to clean the house, cook the dinner, and be my chauffeur."

But no sooner were the words out of my mouth than my subconscious brought me to a screeching halt. Like a bolt of lightning, reality hit me with the thought, *Sheila, you're not the only one feeling burned out*. I had been longing for someone to take care of me in my overload of work and responsibilities—but my family needed someone, too. They still had work and school. They still needed clothes washed, groceries bought, time to be listened to. My working was creating a need in all our lives.

I had become so wrapped up in meeting the demands of the marketplace that I had not clearly seen the effects it was having on those around me. My daughter and I now passed each other in a flurry of activity, our mother-daughter chats few and far between. My son teased me that I was losing my "super-chef" status. When my husband walked in the door, I was no longer his "private listening ear" but an "endless chatter of business jargon." I even felt guilty when a friend told me, "I didn't call because I knew you were too busy."

And if that wasn't enough, my employees were also feeling the pinch of my limited time. I would often look up from my desk to find three people waiting for my undivided attention. I felt pulled in every direction.

My predicament wasn't creating a precedent. I had just joined the ranks of the employed, whose number-one energy guzzler is the effect that relationships have on them. Working women often find themselves straddling an emotional seesaw rocked by conflicts they can't seem to resolve. At one end, they want to give themselves to others in relationship; at the other end, they want to give themselves in their work to accomplish something uniquely their own. They want to reconcile these seeming opposites, not have to choose between them.

One woman I met at a recent retreat recounted an exchange she'd had with her husband as they were walking through an airport. She was exhausted from the week's demands and burdened with thoughts of what was waiting for her when she returned to the office. They passed a gate listing a flight for Hawaii. "That's what I need," she sighed—"a get-away. I don't know if I'd know what to do with myself, but I'd sure like to try."

Her husband slyly remarked, "*I* know what we can do."

The woman told me that when she heard this, "I just wanted to cry. I didn't want a romantic interlude, I wanted isolation!"

She went on to ask me, "How can you be all things, to all people, at all times?"

You can't.

WRESTLING THE GUILT MONSTER

In order to be comfortable with who we are, we have to be confident in the choices we make. Otherwise, the attempt to deal with conflicting situations will only produce internal chaos. Examples abound: The husband who recognizes that his wife must work in order for them to make ends meet, but resents her for surpassing him in the marketplace. The mother who wrestles with being the sole provider of income as well as parental presence. The family members who won't help pick up the slack when Mom must go to work, and Mom who won't delegate and ask for help because she feels she's failing.

The chaos of internal conflicts in relationships is often guilt-inducing. Guilt springs up when we can't be there for others the way we'd like to, and resentment grows when others aren't there for us the way we want them to be. We're constantly trying to maintain a balance between personal needs, professional achievement, and rewarding relationships. But we find we can't do it all at once—and when relationships suffer, it's particularly painful.

This kind of guilt comes in two dimensions. First is the unnecessary burden we often choose to bear.

Think back to when I arrived home to find a supposedly clean house in bedlam. After my moment of lashing out, guilt began to creep in. At first I wanted to carry the burden for everyone. But at that point in time, work was not an option. It was a family commitment.

Feeling guilty or letting others feel sorry for themselves that I was no longer in the "catering" business wasn't going to do anyone any good. It was time to deal with the problem and work together on a solution. Easy? No. Necessary? Yes. It was an essential first step that kept me pushing back the guilt and pulling my family together as a team.

Women who are the sole supporters of their family especially need to resolve the unnecessary guilt that they can't do it all. They need to build their support system on the understanding, "Okay, life's not fair, but together we can turn our circumstances into purposeful living."

The second dimension of relational guilt is the legitimate, diagnostic nudging that signals, "You're out of bounds." It's easy to get so wrapped up in a demanding career in which we're getting constant feedback that we let it take priority over the people who need to experience our presence in their lives.

This legitimate guilt can reveal the need for change by pointing to unhealthy patterns such as workaholism, careerism, and escapism.

Those of us who allow workaholism to stifle relationships are suffering under a load of the wrong priorities. We're not happy unless we're working, because that's where we get all our satisfaction. However unintentionally, we begin to use others as pawns in a game of reaching our work-related goals. Women can get to this point just as easily as men, often at the expense of their closest relationships and their personal health.

Careerism is another pattern that can interfere with satisfying relationships. The quest for identity and achievement, the desire "to be someone," can subtly overtake the value we place on developing healthy bonds with others. This is sometimes a result of misplaced frustration with the quality of personal relationships or dissatisfaction with roles in the home (such as the perception of being "just a homemaker").

When we pursue work at the expense of relationships, it can also point to a pattern of escapism: the attempt to avoid difficulties in relationships through an excessive focus on work, often justified as necessary in order to keep a job or develop a career. This provides an outlet for those who hide their fear of failure in relationships in the simple dismissal, "I just don't have the time."

Finding a solution to this dilemma of resolving the conflicting demands of work and relationships can be a daunting task. But it can be traumatic if we ignore it until it reaches crisis stage. We don't have to wait until we're groaning after the fact to do something about it. We can take charge by seeing relationships as an integral part of personal and professional growth and satisfaction—even more, as one of our basic "reasons for being."

AN ATTITUDE OF GIVE AND TAKE

There's plenty of material available on what makes some relationships flourish and others flounder. What I want to zero in on is understanding how our agendas of career and relationships interface with each other so that we're reducing the chaos in this area of our lives instead of creating it. Part of this understanding is built on the "give and take" of relationships.

Our personal relationships are intricately woven into our career vision. But as they intertwine, we often don't invest energy in confronting the issues that inevitably come up. The crossover effect between our personal and professional lives starts to have negative instead of positive effects: our careers can be undermined by people, and our relationships can be sabotaged by our work.

In order to meet the challenges of resolving conflicts, living with tensions, and relaxing in and enjoying our relationships, it's important that we consciously evaluate how our work life merges with the important people in our personal culture. We can't afford to drift through our relationships without an action-vision that enables us to make consistent choices.

Developing action-vision for relationships requires an understanding of how other people affect us as well as how we influence our relationships. One way to develop this understanding is to look at the mixture of "care-giving" and "care-taking" that we engage in with others. We want to give care to others, but we also need to take the care that others can give us. If we're doing too much care-giving, we get burned out; if we're doing too much care-taking, we're overly dependent.

UNDERSTANDING HOW OTHERS AFFECT US

Recently I went through a period in which it seemed there was an epidemic of chaos in my life. It was almost as if people were lined up to sap my energy, handicap my performance, and put me in a defensive mode. It's one thing to be in the midst of chaotic conditions, but quite another to feel isolated by them.

As I assessed the situation, I realized it wasn't that I resented helping others, but that I was drained because there wasn't anyone there replenishing me. I needed some type of personal input that would help rejuvenate me.

These two factors work together to create a cause-and-effect dynamic in relationships: the output of meeting others' needs triggers our own needs for reinforcement—input from others. Even if it's just a smile.

It's extremely important that we become sensitive to how people affect us and how we can affect them—sometimes without even realizing what we're doing. We all need people to stimulate our growth. As iron sharpens iron, so one person sharpens another, the Bible tells us.[1] But we need to understand that if we can sharpen each other, we can also dull each other's ability to perform.

In order to understand how people connections play an important role in our day-to-day performance and in our general state of well-being, I've characterized "people factors" that set up the input-output scenarios in our relationships. These factors can have the effect of a transfusion of strength or a drain on our resources.

I use the term "marketplace" in these categories of people factors to emphasize the interwoven connections between our relationships and our work. I don't mean that these people are only the ones we meet and interact with on the job. In his book *Renewing Your Spiritual Passion*, Gordon MacDonald uses a similar structure to discuss people who affect our spiritual passion. We'll be looking at people who affect our life in the marketplace—family, friends, co-workers, supervisors, employees.

Marketplace Visionary People (MVP)
MVPs are visionaries who empower our vision. They tap into our abilities and envision how to empower us to use them. They are

caring giants who will cross seemingly insurmountable obstacles to give us a motivational boost.

MVPs are the most active players in our own marketplace vision. The CEO who notices that her best employee is a gifted artist and empowers her to develop her skills is an MVP. So is the nurse who spends extra hours in therapy with a stroke patient to empower him to walk again.

Most people are mirrors, reflecting the moods and emotions of others. MVPs are windows, bringing light to bear on our action-visions, illuminating them, and empowering us to implement them.

Marketplace Partnership People (MPP)

MPPs are promoters who share our vision and keep telling us, "You can do it." They are partners who want to be included in the process of accomplishing our vision. They passionately keep the vision kindled, igniting new opportunities when others have been blocked.

MPPs can be friends who encourage us through supportive actions, colleagues who work closely with us to complete projects, or family members who see our potential and promote our efforts with their support.

In the early stages of our expanded business venture, Archery Center International, Kathy and Leslie became our MPPs. With blood, sweat, and tears (literally all three), we worked together to build a distributorship based on quality service.

MPPs draw forth energy from us, but they do not drain it out of us. Their support for our vision stimulates us to give freely to them, in a healthy give and take. They put the team concept to work for us.

Marketplace Caring People (MCP)

MCPs support us in our vision, but they don't necessarily participate in carrying it out the way MPPs do. MCPs care about us, and so they care about our vision. They encourage us, they defend us, they're sensitive to our needs. They're on the lookout for us, no matter what.

When we have a healthy give and take with an MCP, we ignite each other's passion of purpose. MCPs are found across the whole spectrum of our relationships — professional, family, and personal. No matter what they're engaged in, their caring always comes our way. As a close business associate of mine recently said to me, "There's one common denominator of women in the marketplace. We all need to know that someone cares if we wake up."

Joyce, a professional and friend, is an MCP for me. She listens, encourages, and admonishes. She notices my needs and responds to them as she would want me to do for her. Through the years of our friendship, Joyce has cared enough to be faithful and firm in her support — whether it's meant preparing a meal during a time of crisis, calling in the middle of the day to say "I'm praying," or taking a long walk with me just to listen.

We need MCPs. They calm the inner chaos of our experience in the marketplace.

Marketplace Assistant People (MAP)

MAPs assist our vision only as we ask for their help. They believe in what we're doing but don't initiate active support. They follow wherever we lead, but only when we lead.

Because we need to ask for their support in order to get it, MAPs often require extra energy from us. Working women often complain of MAPs, "Sure I get help, but only if I ask. The responsibility is still on me to make sure everything gets done."

MAPs are often found among employees we supervise or acquaintances with whom we have some personal or professional contact. Sometimes they're family members who don't oppose us but who aren't active in supporting our efforts in the marketplace. I think at times, we all fall into this class.

Kay, a researcher in an economics consulting firm, was assigned to work with Penny on a special project. Penny was thrilled at getting the opportunity to work with Kay and constantly told her how great she was. But Penny only worked on what Kay told her to do. She took no initiative herself to expand on the research.

Penny wasn't lazy; she was a MAP, going where others pushed or pulled her. MAPs do not usually perceive themselves as having a personal stake in what they do.

Marketplace Dependent People (MDP)

MDPs are dependent on us to meet their needs. These relationships especially require careful attention on our part—not only to discern the best way to meet such urgent needs, but also to know when to give freely and when to pull back lest we exhaust ourselves.

In many cases, MDPs' needs are unavoidable—for example, the elderly parent who needs constant care; children; a close friend in severe crisis; a business partner who runs into personal problems and needs us to keep not only our own vision alive but also their vision from collapsing.

I call these people life-cycle MDPs, because their periods of need arise simply as part of the process of their cycle of life events. While their weight is on our shoulders they draw on our energy reserves. But this is the time when we can demonstrate our heartfelt care for them: when they can't stand alone and need a crutch for a while. Even though we may be stressed, there is fruitfulness in giving. And in the back of our mind is the realization that someday we will be in the position of a life-cycle MDP.

But not all MDPs are in this unavoidable category. Some people are just constantly dependent on others to meet their needs. There is always a problem of some kind, and so they live in a perpetual crisis stage from which they continually plead for rescuing. I call these folks constant-cycle MDPs, because their need never goes away. It's not part of life's natural process, but an unnatural state of developmental arrest.

We should be concerned about constant-cycle MDPs and their needs. However, we should not simply feed those needs in an endless stream of giving. This will quickly drain our energy, and the MDPs will still be in need even when we've given all we can.

Recognizing the difference between life-cycle and constant-cycle MDPs can help us understand why we feel overwhelmed.

This understanding will then aid us in deciding on beneficial solutions for how we will respond to the challenges they represent.

Marketplace Sabotage People (MSP)

MSPs undermine what we do, whether unintentionally or deliberately. Ignorance of them isn't bliss; it's a handicap. However painful the process, we need to recognize these people in order to respond effectively to the relationship. MSPs sabotage our efforts by damaging, or even destroying, our vision. Their behavior is most destructive when we are blinded to it.

MSPs can be family members who consciously or unconsciously resent our work; friends or acquaintances who are judgmental of us; business associates who are jealous or threatened or simply incompetent. Toni's boyfriend constantly put down her abilities out of fear that she would overshadow him. Sue had a fierce competitor who personally destroyed her credibility with a client. Kelly's boss was unwilling to give her the authority to implement her vision for improved procedures because he was afraid of losing her to a management position when others noticed her abilities.

Why is it important to understand these different ways in which our relationships affect us? Because it enables us to understand why we can become so drained. As working women, we need to use discernment in reviewing the effects of our relationships. This doesn't mean we should be judgmental, picking and choosing and eliminating based on self-serving criteria. It means there are times when we need to be more of a care-taker than a care-giver. Sometimes we need to seek out people who come alongside us in a supportive way. This is a major part of how we replenish our energies to maintain our care-giving.

It's essential to have a constructive blend of care-taking and care-giving. Then, we'll find that we can give to MAPs and MDPs without expecting anything in return. People change, and so do their interactions with others. Through our caring, we may empower those needy people in our lives to grow in the qualities they bring into relationships.

Because we have no control over how others behave toward

us, our action-vision for our relationships should be based on *who we want to become*. That's why it's important to see ourselves in these "people factors" and use the insights to readjust our behavior to enable us to give transfusions of care to others.

CARE, THE BIGGEST PART OF *CAREER*

Making *care* the biggest part of *career* requires realistic expectations of and insights into who we are and who we can become. It includes words like "limitations," "imperfections," "self-control," and "change" in our understanding of personalities. They may not be enticing words, but they're what make relationships work.

Caring for others involves awareness and honesty regarding how our actions affect them. Although it can be difficult to assess how we treat others and what we need to change, this is what sets the stage for quality giving. If only we could be as honest with ourselves as this writer:

> I am like James and John.
> Lord, I size up other people
> in terms of what they can do for me;
> how they can further my program,
> feed my ego,
> satisfy my needs,
> give me strategic advantage.
>
> I exploit people,
> ostensibly for your sake,
> but really for my own sake.
>
> Lord, I turn to you
> to get the inside track
> and obtain special favors,
> your direction for my schemes,
> your power for my projects,
> your sanction for my ambitions,

> your blank check for whatever I want.
> I am like James and John.
>
> Change me, Lord.
> Make me a [person] who asks of you and of others,
>   what can I do for you?[2]

Our hope for creating a career without creating chaos for others lies in focusing on "Change me, Lord. Not the boss, not my spouse, not my children, but *me*, Lord!" and then trusting God to work in others.

Sometimes, becoming the right person in a relationship means finding where we make mistakes and forging new bonds with the right actions.

John and I found our marriage feeling the effects of our growing business. You might think that the business growth would make life better, but the demands were taking their toll. My leadership position often made it difficult for me to shift gears from work to home. The long hours were exhausting me. I found myself demanding that John meet the needs that I couldn't meet. I became resentful when he couldn't.

But John was in a readjustment stage, too. He was adjusting to changes as he made his new entrance into the business. Even though we were partners, he was in a drastic learning curve of daily routines. We were both struggling for support, and simultaneously feeling drained and isolated.

After some agonizing interludes, I took an attitude of "Change me, Lord." I invited John to a business lunch as my partner. As we talked I told him, "I'm being pulled between the total commitment I have to our marriage and the demands of running a business professionally and profitably. You're the main man at home and my first priority. At the same time, we've made a choice to be partners in business. The conflicts are deteriorating our ability to perform at work and causing stress in our relationship. We need each other. Let's work out a strategy for supportive coexistence and guidelines for performance at the office."

John and I had reached a new stage in our relationship. We

knew what it took to maintain a good marriage. We reaffirmed its priority in our lives and then began transferring the skills we'd used in that agenda to build a firm foundation on which to merge our personal relationship with a joint venture in the marketplace. This meant that we could not only coexist but complement each other.

With the number of family-owned businesses growing by leaps and bounds, many couples are faced with this same situation. But the problem isn't limited to spouses who work together. It crops up any time multiple demands are made on us. Relationships are affected daily by changing circumstances. We must be willing to address these changes with our own willingness to change, to communicate and merge agendas.

My conference with John had a happy ending. But one of the most difficult jobs in caring is accepting the frustrating reality that just because we do the right thing doesn't mean others will respond the right way. We have no control over others' thoughts, beliefs, or actions. We must put our energy into being the right person in a relationship. Then, as constant care flows through us and softens the ego struggles, we can put our "reason for being" into place. We'll find that relationships are part of our purpose — not at cross-purposes with our vision.

How helpful it would be if we could input the necessary data into a computer and have it produce the right formula for each of our relationships. However, people and relationships are controlled not by technology but by tender loving care. Caring relationships don't just happen; they take work. The key to having good relationships lies in our willingness to be the exception.

Caring Means Being Exceptional

Women long for someone to care in today's "who cares?" work environment. There are many hurting people in the marketplace: the mid-life returnee trying to deal with a terrible lack of identity; the distraught single parent craving someone to share the burdens; women who are trying to say "I do" to marriage *and* professional life. Even the young single careerist, who brings such enthusiasm to the marketplace, has a down side: while she proudly proclaims, "My greatest asset is doing what I want to do when I want to do it," she faces the harsh realities of having no one to turn to for support.

Those who feel secure in God's unique plan can find the strength in the midst of struggle to reach out to others. They can stand out as the exception to the "who cares?" operating mode.

Being the exception is a good kind of different. Exceptions care about what happens to others whether they have a personal stake in it or not. They're anchored in their purpose of caring: making the Master more meaningful in the lives of searching, hurting people.

It's an exceptional person who takes the time to understand others' needs, just as she longs to have hers understood. As she looks into the depths of her own needs, she sees how common they are to people in general. When she feels lonely, there is someone else seeking companionship. Because she has fears, she can say to others who are afraid, "I've been there too." The caring person looks beyond what people say, to notice and respond to how they feel.

We all have times when we feel so drained that all we can think of is our own powerlessness, never mind empowering others. *Except*—God does not leave us to our own resources. When we determine to be exceptional in the marketplace, God empowers us:

> He gives strength to the weary and increases the power of the weak. . . . those who hope in the LORD will renew their strength. They will soar on wings like eagles; they will run and not grow weary, they will walk and not be faint.[4]

As God empowers us, He enables us to empower others. *Empowerment is power given to us, so that we can in turn give power to others.* Deep down, all of us know that caring is what makes the difference in being able to empower others. Because we care, we cheer "Don't quit!" when muscles ache, thinking slows down, and the boss makes unrealistic demands.

On the other hand, after a chaotic day at work, it's not the bottom line or the carrot of success that keeps us pressing on. It's the people who care for us, and the people we care for. Business projections may not come true, recognition may quit coming our way, expertise may become obsolete; but the exceptional investments we make in relationships will have eternal significance.

As I've transferred lessons I've learned on relationships from home to marketplace, a big one has been that life is not a decathlon, requiring us to excel in every event. It's more like a medley — in some events we excel, in others we need help. This is an important lesson in caring for others. Being exceptional doesn't mean adding on a bunch of expectations for our behavior. Sometimes, it means turning them loose.

There came a time in my family's growth when I realized that the pattern I had set in my early years of covering up my own shortcomings was having a negative effect on the lives of my children. I felt like a failure.

Then I came across a passage in Scripture that declares, "Though my mother and father forsake me, the LORD will receive me."[5] If I would put my failures and shortcomings in the Lord's hands, He could turn them into stepping stones in the lives of my children.

I realized it was time for me to turn loose the expectations I had of myself, and of my children as well. Where I saw problems, God saw possibilities. How freeing to know that God is in control of our lives — it's not all up to us.

Caring for others becomes a realistic opportunity, not an impossible challenge, when we know Christ's powerful presence is with us. He gives us the power to be exceptional as we merge responsibilities and relationships.

TIMES AND SEASONS

One of the greatest challenges in merging our agendas of career and relationships is reconciling the conflicts between our desire to maintain healthy, enjoyable relationships and our need to devote huge chunks of time and energy to our job.

As the pace of life quickens, it seems to move people in and out of our lives rapidly. If we don't set a priority on relationships, they can slip in and out of our lives. By the time we realize how much we appreciate them, it's sometimes too late to hold on to them.

In order to build and nurture relationships in the midst of a busy schedule, we need to recognize that relationships are not meant to stay the same forever. They have times and seasons; they take on different roles at different times in our lives. This understanding can free us from the either/or choices that sometimes seem forced upon us.

So often we end up facing difficult questions in our relationships: "Why is this happening?" "Will we ever work it out?" "Why do I keep trying?" "Why don't I ever see that special friend anymore?"

The place to start in answering these questions is with our purpose—who we are, and who we want to become. This is the solid basis for our choices, not guilt and pressure and expectations. As we define ourselves within each of our relationships, we can move from there to a vision for what we want from our relationships, what we want to give to them, and why they're important.

To develop an action-vision for a given relationship, I find it helpful to define what I need in that relationship and then let it reflect back to me what I should be giving. This helps me visualize what I can become in the relationship, which is really the only choice I have control over.

For example, I need my family to be there for me. Reflecting back on myself, this means that I need to be there for them. As I realize that I can't be there one hundred percent of the time, I also realize that neither can they. This kind of visualizing "mirrors" what I need to become in the relationship, and it also gives me a realistic perspective. If I'm not aware of what I need, I'm not likely to be aware of what I must be willing to give.

Remembering that relationships flow through times and seasons gives us an overall perspective that can relieve us of unnecessary guilt and yet also remind us to give each relationship the individualized consideration it needs. Developing an action-vision for who we want to become gives us a specific perspective that can guide us in nurturing each relationship according to its unique dynamics and the importance it has in our lives. In chapter 7, we'll look more closely at how synchronizing our steps toward our action-visions gives us the ability to move ahead in all our agendas, without having to sacrifice one to make progress in another.

A VISION FOR RELATIONSHIPS

I recently read about the cabbage rose, a flower that gets its name from its many overlapping petals, which give the appearance of a head of cabbage. This rose is known not for its beauty, but for its toughness and its wonderful fragrance.

This flower brought to my mind a picture of what our relationships should be like — tough (long-lasting, enduring) and fragrant (suffused with the aroma of caring).

Women of action-vision focus on the staying power of relationships. Just as the cabbage rose has overlapping petals that fit smoothly together, so they have overlapping relationships that are in harmony with each other rather than in constant conflict. These women focus not on the beauty of appearances, but on the underlying realities: the toughness of their commitment and the fragrance of their caring. They adopt the attitude, "I want to make a difference in the marketplace without making others pay a price for that difference."

When we determine to be the caring exception, in God's strength we can grow tough enough to withstand adversity without compromise, continuing to send forth the fragrance of love, kindness, patience, truthfulness, and understanding.

Reflect on your relationships. Is there a warmth in them that others can sense? Do you have the toughness to withstand peer pressures to compromise? Are you emitting the fragrance of a caring commitment?

Think about the areas in which you would like to grow. Would you like to be less scattered and more purposeful about your relationships? Should you be less demanding and more uplifting? Check through the "people factors" that characterize your relationships — whether the people you're involved with are encouragers, promoters, care-givers, assistants, dependents, or underminers. Are you drained because you're carrying all your relationships? Perhaps you need to develop the skills of give and take.

Remember that God cares for you. He wants you to get rid of debilitating anxiety and experience the rewards of living out your purpose through relationships. God cares for those people around you. He wants you to reflect Him by drawing others to the fragrance you send out as an exceptional woman in today's marketplace. And He wants you to experience Him in others who reflect Him back to you in the relationships He created you to enjoy.

CHAPTER SIX

TAKE CHARGE WITH CHANGE IN THE MARKETPLACE
▼▼▼▼▼

Never one thing and seldom one person
can make for a success. It takes a number
of them merging into one perfect whole.[1]

Women have come a long way. But they're discovering the risks of making the journey. Chaos is evident everywhere in the marketplace. Women see veils of discrimination but lack the tools to pierce through them. They look for role models but there are few to be found. Their first-class educations have given them the ability to achieve higher performance, but often without better positions or increased wages.

Women are feeling the heavy weight of trying to have it all, all at once. Many women with families, torn between job and home, are singing "I wanna go home."

The twenty-first century will find women composing over half the work force. The U.S. Census Bureau's statistics show that the number of working women has doubled in the last four decades. Yet most of us greet the marketplace with mixed reviews. From the outside looking in, we idealize visions of grandeur. From the inside looking out, we realize what a hostile world the workplace can be.

One woman described the experience in vivid terms: "Entering the work force is like going to a sale. After you wait hours on the fringe of a screaming, pushing mob, you plunge toward the counter with both arms flying." The frantic pace of today's marketplace has made women feel like they're in a "push come to shove" environment.

Going beyond chaos to find order in this environment requires determining what we want to do and how we want to accomplish it. But this is not a simple task. For many of us, it strikes a chord of varying emotions because either we have a mixed bag of feelings about what we want, or we're under pressure from the conflicting reactions of others based on what they want from us.

The majority of working women want to make a significant contribution in the marketplace—whether they're working for financial reasons or simply personal choice. They want to know how to merge into a structured environment and make their presence felt in a positive way.

We've all been struggling with the means to making this positive contribution. The solutions start with getting a realistic picture of what is happening in the marketplace today. I want to focus on two major forces—the Glass Ceiling Phenomenon and the Reeling Effect.

BUMPING UP AGAINST THE GLASS CEILING

The proverbial Glass Ceiling is a perceived barrier that allows women to glimpse, but prevents them from grasping, positions farther up the corporate ladder. It's the point at which they feel discriminated against, and sometimes are.

It's unrealistic to assume that this barrier will simply disappear with time. It will go away only when society transforms its mindset, for that is where the Glass Ceiling is located: in the mind of the perceiver. Sometimes it exists in society "out there," where women have to go against the current of stereotypes and conventional practices. But sometimes it exists in the minds of women themselves, who must break through the assumptions they've been taught in order to open up the possibilities that are truly there.

Jeana, an attractive college administrator, was raised on a farm. She worked hard growing up, performing daily chores side by side with her brother.

One night at the dinner table, Jeana's brother asked their father, "What can I do when I graduate from high school?"

"I see three possibilities for you, son," his father replied. "You can go to college, begin taking over the farm, or look for another job."

Then Jeana asked her father the same question.

"Jeana, I see two possibilities for you," her father answered. "You can get married, or you can get married."

After graduation, Jeana followed her father's lead. During her troubled marriage, she continued her education. When she was thrust into the marketplace by a divorce, she was prepared to provide for herself and her children.

Jeana's Glass Ceiling was society's norm as reflected through her father's views. She eventually saw through that barrier, although it took some hard lessons to do so. Today, she helps other women see through the Glass Ceilings of their own minds through college counseling.

Unfortunately, many women limit themselves mentally by perceiving their roles only in terms of providing support. They can't visualize giving birth to a concept and gathering the support to carry it through to completion. For these women, the Glass Ceiling Phenomenon is largely self-made.

How should we perceive the Glass Ceiling? Certainly not as a limitation, for then we fall into the trap that will keep us in an unhealthy mindset. We should look at the Glass Ceiling, no matter who put it there, as a challenge to grow — to burst through it or detour around it, depending upon the circumstances.

If we perceive obstacles as limitations, we will be blocked from accomplishing our goals. But if we decide to look through and beyond obstacles, we can turn them into opportunities for growth. If we're not qualified, we can increase our capabilities. If we're short on communication skills, we can develop them. If we're weak in decision-making, we can practice our conceptual skills.

Sometimes we'll discover that the Glass Ceiling is not in our minds, but a reality in our organization. In this case we can use the knowledge as leverage to change course or to clarify the reasons for remaining where we are. Through understanding our purpose for being in an organization, we can become content in situations we would otherwise rebel against.

When we are purpose-empowered, we understand that we are in the marketplace for reasons other than advancement. This knowledge enables us to see the Ceiling from a different vantage point. For example, we can view it as protective — perhaps there's a good reason for remaining in a given position, even though it creates a plateau. Or we can view it as a signpost for detouring us into a new marketplace because we are deadlocked where we are. Sometimes, the Glass Ceiling works to our benefit by keeping us from overextending ourselves during certain stages in our lives.

Each of us has our own structure of needs and wants from which we make decisions about our place in the work force. Some women have the option of providing the second income but choose not to exercise it because of other priorities. Others are forced by circumstances to aid in financial support but do not seek advancement because of family commitments. For women who do pursue a career path, the key to breaking through the Glass Ceiling may be to chip away at the doubts of predisposed minds in order to propel themselves through the opportunities offered in the marketplace. Perceptions can't be controlled, but they can be influenced.

In addition to the Glass Ceiling Phenomenon, a second force affecting women in the marketplace today is the Reeling Effect — when change plus apprehension equals uncertainty.

THE REELING EFFECT

The effects of constant change, combined with our apprehensions about our work, often leave us reeling. Our emotions fluctuate between opposing feelings about the marketplace: "I want to work" versus "When am I going to be able to quit?" When we're on the job, one minute we're thinking, "This project is so exciting!" and the next we're wondering, "How am I ever going to survive this pressure?" As we look at our contribution, satisfaction that we're having a good effect is undermined by anxiety over the chaos we're caught up in. Our contradictory feelings keep us in a state of uncertainty.

These fluctuating emotions characterize the Reeling Effect. It's like getting caught up in a whirlwind and losing our sense of direction.

Our purpose often gets lost in the shuffle of our ambivalence. Emotions swing us from enjoying the rewards of working to fearing the demands. We become blinded to the opportunities to counteract obstacles.

For many women, indecisiveness arises when they simply occupy a job slot instead of effectively creating a career path. A job is accepting a task that has to be done. A career is the pursuit of results that have a long-term significance, even if that pursuit is on a short-term basis.

If I go to work just because I have a job, it confines my perspective to a narrow slice of reality. The phrase "just a job" conjures up unpleasant associations: mundane assignments, boring routines, something to be endured. In this kind of environment, our feelings are bound to fluctuate with daily activities in an aimless moodiness. All too soon we start asking, "What now?" When we're not sure what we're accomplishing or what the ground rules are for doing it, and we receive a meager paycheck to boot, we'll continue to question whether we made the right choice.

But women who are trapped in entry-level jobs are not the only ones suffering from the clash of expectations and reality. Even women on a career track are often caught off-guard with what they find in the marketplace. There doesn't seem to be much security or continuity in many fields. Those who change positions must merge previous skills with new procedures. On-the-job training also means reevaluating direction. College students quickly learn that book knowledge is not enough; the "real world" is more demanding and less forgiving than the more loosely-structured campus scene.

Women often find that staying on the competitive edge means treacherous climbing rather than sustaining accomplishments. The thrill of a new challenge gives way to the agony of moving too fast to be adequately prepared. We thought we knew what we wanted, but once we get it we're not sure it's what we had in mind.

The Reeling Effect keeps us frustrated over the constant effort to prove ourselves, the energy required to avoid unnecessary confrontations with others, and the enduring stress of having to maintain high-quality performance. The stress can reach the point where even if we do love work, we want out anyway. The pleasure of accomplishment is just not worth the struggle for survival.

I took a survey in which I asked women their reasons for working. Some emphasized their desire to make a significant contribution on the job. Many of their responses were along the lines of, "It's what I've always wanted to do." But the biggest percentage of responses were non-career-oriented. These women gave answers such as:

"I don't have any choice."

"I always knew I would work until I got married and had children."

"I was tired of staying at home."

"It seemed exciting at first, but now I'm trapped."

"I needed the income to cover a major expenditure" (such as a house).

When I read these responses, I found myself wondering just how many women had gone to work to buy a new car but then stayed on the job throughout the entire life of the vehicle.

I also asked these women how long they expected to stay in the work force. The majority of women indicated that either they had already been working for a long time or expected to be working far into the future. But in this area, again, their answers were unfocused:

"Until I get tired of it."

"No longer than I have to."

"Until my husband retires."

"Until I have children."

"I don't know. Sometimes I like it, sometimes I don't."

These answers provide good examples of the ambivalence that keeps us reeling with uncertainty. Most women are working because of contingencies, not because of a commitment to a specific plan or vision. In this situation, they will continue to suffer from the Reeling Effect.

The issue of the Glass Ceiling Phenomenon will carry over into the next decade, but it is the Reeling Effect that will be paramount. This force is creating chaos because it resides in working women, not in corporate America. It can't be legislated against, nor can companies protect their investment from it. Women are becoming the heartbeat of the marketplace. Society necessitates their presence. Our nation's business strength depends in large part on the skilled labor that women bring to the business community. The economics of daily living are threatening the job of homemaking with extinction.

Without a vision and opportunistic strategies, the working world will keep women reeling. As the ambivalence of working women increases, so does the chaos of the marketplace. Many women are unwittingly blocking their vision and contribution with indecisiveness and lack of vision.

Perhaps we're entering the closing decade of the twentieth century with a heightened sensitivity to the problems. That's all well and good, but we must go beyond that. It's time to synchronize our assumptions of "what must be" with our desires for "what I want to be," instead of just living for "that day when I can. . . ." Our vision of what ought to be should shape the quality of our life and influence the environment of the marketplace.

But developing a vision isn't the norm for most working women. They wait for the workplace to decide for them which route to take. A major problem with this approach is that companies are in business to make money, not to pave the way for individual career paths. A marketplace action-vision can help uncover solutions that will enable women to communicate their abilities, pursue their aspirations, and demonstrate the value of their work. It will steady them against the dizzying pull of the Reeling Effect.

REAL LIVING IN A REELING WORLD

A major component in developing a vision is the commitment to bringing it to fruition. When we make this commitment and strive to keep it, we begin to experience real living in a reeling world.

Commitment supplies the real value for our vision. It keeps us from being tossed around by the fluctuating circumstances of the marketplace. If we didn't have commitment, we'd be tempted to abandon or radically change our vision every time we hit a rough spot—and we all know that life has plenty of those! Commitment provides the core of achievement. It starts with a state of mind and then shows itself in actions.

Committing ourselves to a vision has many benefits. It keeps us from being self-centered by calling us back from an individualistic freedom to "go with the flow." It injects meaning into our work, taking the "just" out of "just a job." It frees us to give willingly instead of reluctantly.

Our vision becomes reality as commitment turns concepts into creative actions. We must be careful, however, to distinguish commitment from overcommitment. Overcommitment occurs when we don't know when to say when. If we're so committed that we overtax ourselves, we become blinded rather than empowered by the vision. We no longer see the toll it's taking on our health, career, and relationships. This is especially true when we're performing multiple roles simultaneously.

Here is the criterion I use for determining the difference between commitment and overcommitment: the ability to merge other aspects of our life with what we are committed to. A healthy commitment to career will not damage our commitment to relationships and our own personal needs.

DEVELOPING A MARKETPLACE VISION

I want to get you thinking now about what *your* vision for your contribution to the marketplace can be. In the next chapter we'll be exploring how to synchronize our various agendas and move forward a step at a time. But right now I'd like to stimulate you to consider what kinds of action-visions you could be developing for your career.

To get you started, I'll be asking you a series of questions. Don't worry about coming up with answers right away. As you think through the issues that these questions address, you'll be making progress in customizing your plan for becoming a woman of purpose.

**(1) What is it that you really want
to accomplish through your involvement in the marketplace?**
"Far and away the best prize that life offers," said Theodore Roosevelt, "is the chance to work hard at work worth doing." A fortunate few have a clear picture of what their worthwhile work is—it almost seems that picture has been transmitted in their genes.

But this awareness is not the case with many of us. The rest of us are searchers—searching for a job we can truly call a *career* because we care about what we're doing. Even if we try to keep our passion of purpose foremost in our thoughts, we can easily lose sight of what we're working for in the midst of daily turmoil, confrontations with family, and office headaches.

Has your work become a daily struggle? If you're thoroughly frustrated, you'll find it difficult to keep your sights on opportunities and your purpose well-defined.

The key to living in expectation rather than frustration is developing a vision and committing yourself to acting on it. Visualize what you want to do in the marketplace—what you want out of it, what you want to give to it. Then clarify what you are willing to commit to and what you are not. It's important that you determine whether your ambitions are realistic for this phase in your life.

Once you begin to identify what you want to commit yourself to accomplishing, it's time to put together—without illusion and without pessimism—a blueprint of your action-vision based on these criteria: how your work will benefit others; how it expresses your purpose; and how it empowers you to express yourself.

Linda, a devoted wife and mother, found herself returning to work after years of being a full-time homemaker. Her husband's seasonal work required the supplement of a second income in the family.

As Linda began her job search, she made flexibility an essential component in any employment. Her family was still her top priority. She studied for and obtained her real estate license and took a position with a brokerage that understood her commitment to family. As a result of her commitment at work, she won associate-of-the-month awards and became a member of the million dollar club.

Linda's career benefits her employer with quality work. It benefits her family with needed financial support. It allows her to express her purpose in being the parent and spouse she wants to be (and a very dear friend to me!). At the same time, Linda's career allows her to express herself through using her strong people skills.

Linda's career can grow with her desire for further involvement. The position meets her needs now and can adjust to meet changing needs in the future. She accomplished this through a careful, conscious approach to her work. Suppose she had simply drifted into the work force and taken "just a job" to work for "just a paycheck"; she would have been creating chaos in many areas of her life. Instead, Linda took charge with change.

Committing ourselves to a realistic vision and adapting it to fit our specific circumstances keeps us from the constant "close, but not quite there" twilight zone of accomplishment. Check your current involvement in the marketplace against your original desire for work: are you still moving toward it? Or have you bumped up against a Glass Ceiling or lost your sense of direction in the Reeling Effect? Don't be afraid to make mid-course corrections—now is always a good time to start!

(2) What specifications should you be establishing for your marketplace participation?

Once you know the direction you want to head in, it's time to start thinking about the specifics of what your vision will entail.

What do you need in a job, and what are you willing to give? For example, consider these questions:

- Do you want to be able to work: part-time? full-time? temporary?
- What level of challenge would be best for you: significant responsibility? a "no-brainer"? (Either answer can be the right one as long as you're willing to accept the conditions that come with the territory.)
- Do you want your career involvement to be: long-term? short-term?
- In your job experience so far, have you: tried to climb the ladder too fast? lacked achievement or neglected to establish motivating goals because of the Reeling Effect?

Another helpful exercise for customizing your marketplace action-vision is to imagine that you are the employer, and then decide what type of position you will give yourself. The response you come up with here will indicate what degree of commitment you're prepared to make.

When we're consciously aware of what we want and of what is best for those close to us, we can control the chaos instead of being overwhelmed by it. Michelle, a heads-up career woman, began developing her vision in college. Early in her college years she committed herself to preparing for a lifelong career. She evaluated areas of opportunity for women to break ground. Because she identified the direction she wished to take, she was able to merge her personal relationships with her marketplace vision.

Today Michelle is a very successful chemical engineer with a supportive, non-competitive husband. They have scheduled their work patterns together in the best interests of each other and their two children. Michelle's ability to synchronize her agendas, moving forward in all of them at the same time, comes from having a clear picture of what she wanted to accomplish combined with the commitment to build it step by step.

(3) Are you being careful
to discern what really matters in work and life?

Creating a career without creating chaos is built in part on "making a difference without making someone else pay the price." But here we should also add, "without paying too big a price yourself." Even the most enjoyable job can turn sour if we've lost sight of our priorities.

Frieda, a single woman, planned to marry someday and take the "mommy track." For now, she figured, she could take on a position that ate up a lot of her time, because as a single person she could afford its intense demands.

The job Frieda accepted required a lot of travel. At first, it was exciting. Only after she had invested several years in the position did she realize that advancement in her career was costing her personal relationships. She was never in the same place long enough to allow a relationship to grow. Unintentionally, she was sabotaging her desire to get married someday.

Frieda had consigned her relational priorities to the future and allowed her work to usurp their place in her life. In this respect her career choice hampered rather than contributed to fulfilling her long-term desires. Her experience illustrates why we must keep the important priorities foremost in our minds when we make choices. We need to discern what really matters to us and adjust our vision according to long-term ramifications, not just short-term gratification.

Working mothers are increasingly sensitive to evaluating priorities in their decisions about career. This kind of evaluation helps avoid simply being torn between going to work or staying home with children. When a woman's work is in the best interests of her family, she shouldn't waste energy on needless guilt trips or wishful thinking. If work is an option, however, and she finds herself vacillating about it, she should consider alternatives.

These alternatives to the either/or conflict of working versus staying at home are on the rise as women seek flexible solutions. For example, mothers on career paths are increasingly opting for "sequencing" — a detour off the fast-track of a developing career for a few years to concentrate on parenting. Other women have discovered free-lance work, part-time jobs, or entrepreneurship as successful ways to create a career contoured to their specific needs.

(4) How does what you want to accomplish fit into what you're doing now?

Before assuming that you have to start from scratch in implementing your marketplace action-vision, look carefully at how you might build outward from your current situation.

One way to do this is to make sure you are maximizing your contribution in your current position, whether or not it seems to have a clear connection to your vision. When you focus on what more you can do to benefit your organization, you may create possibilities you otherwise wouldn't have.

Julie, a vivacious and caring customer service manager, had a vision to quit work and stay at home when she became a mother. In the meantime, she put in her best efforts at her position. The company benefited from their investment in her through her positive influence on customers and colleagues. Julie reaped financial benefits as well as a sense of accomplishment.

When the time came for Julie to resign her position and turn to full-time mothering, she found that her employer and her customers were enthusiastic about her plans. Her company had been so pleased with her performance that they left the door open for her to come back if she wanted to.

Because of her commitment to maximizing her contribution, Julie took home the satisfaction of accomplishment and recognition as well as the assurance of a reentry point into the marketplace whenever she was ready.

Another way to fit what you're doing now into where you want to go is to consider customizing your action-vision in your current organization. Look at your preferences for work. We normally excel in areas of preference, even over expertise. See if there are any potential openings in your areas of preference. If so, find out what you need to do to qualify for those positions, and let your employer know about your desire to pursue them.

We get high returns on our investment in work. Even if our

position is short-term, we can make a significant contribution that will have lasting results within the organization. The bottom line in this investment is whether we care about our work. Caring is what activates the "commit" in commitment.

(5) How can you tailor your plans for career or work to fit your marketplace action-vision?

There are three keys to thriving in the midst of a chaotic marketplace: knowing what you're trying to accomplish; setting realistic expectations for what you will achieve; and staying committed to your purpose.

Now that you've begun thinking about what you want to accomplish, evaluate that thinking. What do you personally want to get out of your employment? What challenges do you face? What is generating your greatest frustration? Where does the biggest gap occur between what you *are* doing and what you *want* to be doing? What resources do you have now for making changes? How do your plans for career merge with your other agendas for meeting personal needs and maintaining relationships?

Use the issues raised by these questions to adjust your vision for your contribution in your work. Look at what you're doing now to see how it might enable your progress toward your goals—or to see how you need to change what you're now doing in order to clear away obstacles you have control over.

Once you begin to identify a marketplace action-vision, commit yourself to it—even if it's in the incubator stage. It's an opportunity. It's a beginning. Don't let doubts force you into retreat—it's better to have expectations that are too high than no expectations at all. As Frederic Amiel counseled, "The [woman] who insists upon seeing with perfect clearness before [she] decides, never decides. Accept regret." Revise your vision, but don't give up.

THE GENIE IN THE BOTTLE

The marketplace is in a constant state of change. In order to take charge in this environment instead of being swept along by the forces at work in it, we need to set our sights with action-vision. Then we need to carry out that vision a step at a time (how to do this is the subject of the next chapter) and make progress in the midst of chaos. By keeping purpose as the cornerstone for our marketplace blueprint, we'll avoid selecting the wrong responses to change or implementing the right responses in the wrong way.

But many women live like a genie trapped in a bottle—a lot of potential with no place to go. They know there are obstacles creating chaos but don't know how to conquer them. They feel restless and unsatisfied, knowing there must be more "out there" but unsure of how to get to it.

These women see what is going on around them and have the power within them to do something about it, but they're trapped because of what they perceive controls them. They can see through the glass container that's confining them, but they can't pop off the cap.

We may not have a genie's magical power, but we do have the resources God created us with and the strength He has promised to give us. As we build our approach to the marketplace on the foundation of commitment, and make daily choices based upon our purpose-empowered action-vision, we will release our potential from its confinement. The Glass Ceiling and the Reeling Effect limit us only if we allow them to.

As we learn how to channel our power to take charge with our work, we will benefit others around us as we express our individualized purpose. Being a Christian woman in the marketplace is not a classification but a customized application of Christ living through us day by day. It is sending out a glow, not a glare, that lights the path of those searching for meaning.

When we see beyond the chaos of the marketplace to the bottom line, it is not the pressure of a position but a passion of purpose. That's when we can achieve extraordinary results one step at a time with eternal significance.

PART THREE

PROGRESS
IN THE MIDST
OF CHAOS

Achieving Extraordinary Results
One Step at a Time

▼▼▼▼▼▼

CHAPTER SEVEN

SYNC OR SINK: INTEGRATING YOUR AGENDAS WITH MINI STEPS

▼▼▼▼▼▼

*People with goals succeed because they
know where they are going.*[1]

I vividly remember riding past a golf course on a windy, cold spring day and wondering, *What makes intelligent people do something as ridiculous as chasing a little ball over miles of grass? I would never do that!*

Well, "never" came last Saturday. That's right—I was one of those half-crazy people, fighting the wind and cold to show that willful little ball that I could do what I came to do: get it in the hole, regardless of the wind.

We golfers (see how fast our perspectives change?) are funny creatures—and sometimes less than honest, especially about why we play golf. I've heard every reason in the world, and I think they're all up for question.

Just think about it from a rational point of view. Golfers say they want exercise, but then they drive around the course in this goofy little cart with a parasol over it. During the long, hot days of summer, golfers moan and groan if the office temperature isn't within two degrees of the comfort zone, but they think nothing of playing outdoors in 105 degree weather. Golfers say they play for relaxation, but they have a conniption if they don't take five strokes off their score every time they play.

So, why *do* we play? Perhaps the game provides an escape from work-related inner conflicts—the insecurity of not being able to score our performance and the fear that even when we do our best, it's not enough. Judging ourselves against the beautifully simple standard of how many strokes it takes to place an insignificant ball into a ridiculously tiny hole is a whole lot easier than trying to measure ourselves according to the subjective standards and quirky circumstances of our professional world.

In the last three chapters we've focused on envisioning what we want to accomplish in three key agendas—personal, relationships, and marketplace. Once we establish vision, we need to move forward in a process that will enable us to reach our objectives.

In the world of work, knowing what you want to accomplish and judging your effectiveness at it can be frustrating. When someone asks us, "How did your day go?" we often convince ourselves according to the emotions of the moment—it was "great," "pretty good," "not bad," or "awful"—rather than relying on a way to evaluate our progress.

To avoid a subjective—and therefore frustrating—evaluation of how we progress in achieving our visions, we need to set forth specific objectives we wish to accomplish in the order they need to be done.

In golf, the objective is to finish the course. However, it is accomplished hole by hole. To carry out our visions for who we become and what we accomplish, we must develop a course of action *step by step* in order to finish the course without losing our sense of direction.

PLAN FOR CHANGE

If you watch the haphazard path that some golfers take—through the woods, into the ponds, buried in the sand traps—you might think they're confused. Some of the problems are caused by bad technique; others are due to the complexity of the course. Golfers can improve their technique and become more knowledgeable about the course, but they can't control the changing conditions that affect how the course is played, such as ever-changing winds and fluctuating weather, or the greenskeeper's positioning of the pin.

The same process is true with our vision. We can hone our vision carefully and study the surrounding environment, but we have no control over most changes.

Change comes in many configurations. One type of change alters priorities—having a child, starting a relationship, beginning a new job. Another type of change is the sort that you know is coming—buying a house, getting an education, growing older. Then there are the unexpected changes—financial difficulty, a troubled marriage, a new boss at work.

Changes often occur at inopportune times, when we're right in the middle of something and wish the changes would occur only on *our* timetable. But it just doesn't happen that way. However, we *do* have control over our response to change, and we do influence how change affects us. We can become more knowledgeable by creating opportunistic strategies that enable us to respond more effectively.

Opportunistic strategies give us the foresight to be prepared and enable us to develop the right techniques for action. They are characterized by flexibility. If our action-visions are too rigid we'll find ourselves frustrated from lack of achievement, perhaps ready to throw in the towel on the vision itself. In the fast-paced business world, the "I'm going to do it no matter what" mindset just isn't realistic.

John F. Welch, Jr., CEO of General Electric, transformed the company from a bureaucracy to one of today's most forward-looking corporations. He made this prediction about the business environment:

> The pace of change in the nineties will make the eighties look like a picnic—a walk in the park. Competition will be relentless. The bar of excellence in everything we do will be raised every day. The pace of change will be felt in every area.[2]

The pace of change will be felt in all our agendas. It always affects our strategies because there are too many "moving parts" for us to control. Therefore, our achievements are dependent not only upon the right assets, but upon putting those assets to use with a focused effort in a timely manner. I once told an employee, "It's not only how we handle what is happening now, but how we handle the changes to come that will decide our success."

However threatening it may seem, change is not a bad thing in itself. It gives life a spicy flavor—without it, we'd become lackadaisical and bored. Whether change is a godsend or a curse depends on whether we're moving with it or struggling to catch up to it. We can make the difference with realistic strategies for achievement.

MINI STEPS: A WORKING WOMAN'S PLAN

Realistic strategies are composed of short-term, attainable goals that will move us toward our visions. Without these steps along the way, we'd never be able to make the journey. I call these planning nuggets MINI Steps—Moving In Natural Increments. These specific steps keep us moving purposefully through the chaos. They are the "action" part of action-vision.

In his book *Self-Renewal*, John Gardner states that the only stability possible is "stability in motion."[3] This phrase is a good description of what our lives look like when we're anchored by purpose and moving forward toward vision. MINI Steps coordinate that forward movement in the midst of change, utilizing three key components: *agility, anticipation*, and *adaptability*.

Agility is the mental ability to respond quickly and resourcefully. This quality empowers us to assess the circumstances around us, weigh our options, and respond—even if we're caught between contradictory forces, or the pros and cons of the variables we're dealing with. Mental agility keeps our thoughts clear without narrowing us into shortsightedness. This effect increases our decisiveness.

Connie, a sales manager for a women's wear company, found out that her next promotion was dependent upon increased sales during the off-season. She had good reason to believe that this condition had been imposed on her because her supervisor was threatened by her current level of success. Connie would have to respond quickly or her career plans would be greatly hindered.

Connie came up with creative ideas and put them into action. First, she instituted a sales competition with her employees to get them behind her. Second, she examined her own behavior to detect any wrong signals she might have been giving to her supervisor. She identified two issues in which she'd acted rashly and rectified the situations. Because she responded quickly and put her resources to work, Connie stayed on track with her career.

Anticipation is the ability to think ahead. It is preparing for the future without being controlled by it. What frightens many of us about change is not knowing what will happen next and what it will take to get through it. Anticipation allows us to project what the specific effects of change will be on our plans, and then take the course of action that will be to our greatest benefit when the change does occur. This quality gives us the understanding we need to adjust plans and priorities according to how we perceive change will affect them.

Sue was offered an opening in another department of her company. It involved more pay without any apparent increase in responsibility level. It seemed like a great opportunity.

Before making a decision, Sue looked ahead to anticipate how the change would affect her. Her current supervisor was likely to receive a promotion in the near future, and the only person in that same department with more seniority than Sue would be retiring soon. Sue decided not to take the offer of a transfer to another department. Her anticipation paid off as she moved rapidly through the company.

Anticipation tailors our strategies to change. It can open our eyes to alternate routes or show us why to stick to our current target.

Adaptability is the ability to modify our behavior to meet various changing circumstances. It enables us to be versatile in our approaches without changing our vision. It also helps us to initiate change, exchange old habits for new ones, and integrate new responsibilities with existing tasks.

Adaptability is what enables working women to handle more than one role. We can be the homemaker yet still become the professional. Each requires a unique set of behaviors, thought patterns, and skills. When we're adaptable, we can transfer skills or abilities from one role to the other. Home management skills, for example, can be translated for professional application in the marketplace.

MINI Steps are effective when we use our mental agility to help us respond quickly to change by anticipating its effects. Our adaptability puts these responses into action with the right behavior at the right time. When these components are all operating together, our plans will Move In Natural Increments.

Building strategies with MINI Steps requires that we use the following tools: *Milestones*, which are targets for our short-term goals; *synchronization*, our mode of movement forward; and *feedback*, our scoring system that enables us to evaluate our progress.

MILESTONES

To take charge of what we accomplish, rather than just leaving it to chance, we must plan for it. Just like the holes on a golf course, we need points of reference that demonstrate our progress. I call these reference points *Milestones*, because they mark advances along the way in our progress toward vision.

Milestones give us a sense of accomplishment and a natural reevaluation point to reaffirm or revise our strategy for the next significant development.

I'm not referring here to the complicated, guilt-inducing goal-setting so many women have grown to know and despise. Before I discovered the benefits of MINI Steps and Milestones, my goal-setting was like a table-setting. I'd put the utensils on the table in the right place, and very soon they would be moved around, messed up, and then put away in the sink or dishwasher, to be forgotten until next time I took them out. It was the same with my goals: I'd put them down on paper in the right way, but it didn't take long for them to be messed up. Then I'd put them away and forget about them until out of guilt or desperation or yet another earnest attempt to make it work I would take them out and start all over again. This frustrating pattern would repeat itself: write goals, drift away from my plans, rewrite my goals.

This cycle of non-progress turned me off to traditional goal-setting. Now I Move In Natural Increments, using Milestones to mark my progress toward accomplishing my ultimate vision. A goal is the end toward which effort is directed; a Milestone is a significant point of development in that effort.

Using Milestones makes it easier to work toward goals because they set a point of accomplishment that is ahead but within reach. We can concentrate our efforts on reaching that point without becoming overwhelmed by trying to focus on the whole picture at one time. Movement will occur more effectively when we take small, decisive steps rather than trying to span too much distance in one leap. Sometimes we'll have to extend our strides, but it shouldn't be beyond our natural limitations.

Milestones give us feedback along the way by letting us know we're making progress. They don't mean we've "arrived," but they take away the sense of discouragement or failure that we haven't *yet* "arrived."

I learned the importance of Milestones on family trips when our children were young. My nerves got set on edge each time I heard them ask, "How much farther do we have to go, Mom?" — they repeated it about every five minutes! Was it ever *great* when they were old enough to understand milestones. Then marking our progress became a game. I pointed out the milestones on the route and explained they showed how far we had come. This gave them a tool to judge how our position was changing.

To use the journey analogy, if the destination is our goal, then the routes we take to get there are MINI Steps. The land-marks along the way are Milestones.

For example, let's say that as part of my vision for quality years with my husband after the children are grown, I make it my goal to spend time regularly with him in creative and high-quality ways. Now I need to plan what steps I will take to reach that goal. I decide to set a Milestone to spend three uninterrupted hours per week with him. After discussing this with John, I will write into my schedule whatever actions are necessary to reach that weekly Milestone — having lunch once a week, coffee on Saturday morning, a Sunday afternoon walk, and so on.

HOW TO TAKE THOSE FIRST FEW STEPS

To get started in Moving In Natural Increments, we need to move from our purpose to our visions. Once we establish visions in our personal priorities, relationships, and professional development, we can formulate MINI Steps.

Start by establishing small, decisive steps that will move you toward your vision. For example, you could set aside time on your calendar, a half hour each month, to decide on monthly steps in your three agendas. Attach deadlines to these steps. If they require daily action, write in those actions on your calendar. Use Milestones to mark significant development points (perhaps one each week per agenda) along the way — and when you reach them, share them with a good friend who will celebrate your accomplishments and encourage you to keep at it. At the end of each month, evaluate your development, clarify your expectations, and move on to the month ahead.

Your Milestones are helpful targets that give structure to your MINI Step plan. Once you establish weekly Milestones in your once-a-month planning session, you'll know how to fill in the tasks or activities that will move you from one Milestone to the next. Here are ten suggestions that can help you in creating a MINI Step plan:

1. *Change your attitude about goal-setting.* Look at Milestones as personal points of development in reaching your vision.

2. *Focus on the next Milestone.* Don't be distracted by the overall picture. Stick to the issue at hand.

3. *Avoid procrastination.* Putting things off is usually another way of saying, "There's an obstacle keeping me from taking the next step." If there is an obstacle, work at eliminating it. If there isn't,

determine to overcome your reluctance and take the next step.

4. *Be open to alternatives.* Preconceived notions can limit your options. Use mental agility, anticipation, and adaptability to keep you moving forward.

5. *Give yourself immediate feedback.* Your vision will not turn into reality overnight, so you need the reinforcement of jobs well done along the way. Congratulate yourself each time you successfully complete a step.

6. *Stay committed, even when you stumble.* One step always leads to another. If you veer off track, use Milestones to get you back on track. Work from where you are, not from where you think you should be.

7. *Be willing to risk small failures in order to achieve big gains.* View stumbling blocks as potential stepping stones. Learn from your experience, and congratulate yourself for trying. Then try again.

8. *Champion your own cause.* Don't let people with negative attitudes block your progress. Adjust your own sails, seek God's guidance, and move ahead, looking for innovative ways to accomplish your next step.

9. *Think big.* Go back to your overall vision for inspiration and a reminder of why you're in the daily challenges. Use your vision as a blueprint for long-term, sustained effort.

10. *Keep your Milestones short and simple.* Don't set your landmarks so far out ahead of yourself that you'll have trouble reaching them. If your Milestones are too ambitious, they may be outmoded by the time you get anywhere near them—if you can even stay on course that long. Use realistic Milestones with accompanying target dates to plan the steps that will keep you Moving In Natural Increments.

SYNCHRONIZATION: OUR MODE OF MOVEMENT

Life would be easier if we had only one agenda at a time to deal with. But that's not the case. Today's professional woman has personal needs, professional development, and quality relationships to keep attending to all at once. She needs a way to *synchronize* her movements so that she is taking steps on a daily basis to move forward in all agendas.

"He who every morning plans the transaction of the day and follows out that plan," said Victor Hugo, "carries a thread that will guide him through the maze of the most busy life. But where no plan is laid, where the disposal of time is surrendered merely to the chance of incidence, chaos will soon reign."[4]

MINI Steps will sharply reduce haphazard movement by empowering us to coordinate our agendas.

I know what you're thinking right now — *I've tried this before! Even when I make plans, I still can't keep my life balanced!* I agree. Frustration and failure are words that come to mind when we think of the balancing act that women try to perform. Just the *word* "balance" is enough to conjure up negative images: walking a tightrope; scales that measure precisely whether you're in balance or off-balance; bank statements and a checkbook ledger that must be in perfect agreement (with a thousand different possibilities for why they're not!). These examples are bad enough — how can we ever balance our *lives*? No wonder we get frustrated.

The agendas of our life will never be in perfect harmony with each other. They're not equal to each other, and we can't balance them. What we really need is to keep moving forward, personally and professionally, without leaving anything important behind — even though we may have to emphasize one agenda over another at any given time. This is what I mean by *synchronization*.

Synchronization gives us an entirely different picture than balance. Visualize the rhythmic movements of synchronized swimmers as they move through the water. Although each swimmer does not always perform the same exact act as the other, they move together in harmony. Their simultaneous performance is a joy to watch.

That effect is what we can have as we move through the marketplace — a skilled performance, based on a combination of individual movements that work together to create a harmonious whole.

People working or traveling together often synchronize their watches in order to accomplish many different tasks while all staying on the same schedule. We synchronize our agendas so we can merge them smoothly.

Synchronization involves simultaneous movement, not adding a little here and subtracting a little there to strike some idealized balance. I think of it like walking: at any given moment one leg is leading the way, but it doesn't mean that leg is more important than the other. The other leg is right behind, stabilizing the leading leg.

For certain periods of time, one agenda may be leading the way, but that doesn't mean we're leaving the other agendas out of our lives. We carry out different plans in each of them, but we synchronize those plans so that we can keep all of them going simultaneously. This is what gives us stability and support for our forward movement.

Another way to visualize synchronization is to imagine an orchestra performing. Some instruments dominate, others have a lesser role, but all are essential. The many different sounds combine to form a beautiful whole. The printed score provides the plan; the conductor synchronizes the musicians according to that plan.

We make plans based on which agenda takes priority and when. This doesn't mean that if we give one area of our lives priority, we're neglecting all the other areas—that's where so much of our unnecessary guilt comes from. If circumstances dictate that work provides our sole financial support, then it must take priority. This may not be what we *want* to do, but sometimes we have to make tough choices in order to keep our priorities the deciding factors in decision-making. But when we synchronize our agendas, the tough choices don't mean we get rid of other agendas—they just assume a lower-profile role.

Milestones are what give us the specifics to focus on in each agenda. When we write our Milestones down and approach them in a systematic way—by looking at them together and making adjustments in order to fit the individual pieces into a whole scheduling picture—we'll find that synchronizing agendas is more and more like walking. It will come naturally.

Sylvia's vision for her personal growth was to become an

artist. It seemed impossible: she was a single parent with two children to support. It wasn't until Sylvia wrote up her MINI Steps that she realized she did *not* have to give up her vision for art. Because she was the sole support for her children, Sylvia's job had to be a top priority. However, she found that by developing Milestones in each area, she could synchronize quality time for her children with her creative pursuits.

Sylvia's plan included goals in the areas of job, family, and personal growth. Her vision at work was to be a department manager. She developed a plan that included Milestones for skill development in the areas of communication, organization, and leadership.

Sylvia's vision for her children was to spend quality time with them. She set a Milestone for a children's hour three times a week, which was solely for them. Then she designated household responsibilities that her children shared with her rather than each doing tasks individually; these became teaching times in which the children shared responsibility and the accompanying glow of accomplishment. They also provided additional time together.

Sylvia's Milestones included time set aside each week to pursue her art. Although she couldn't attend art classes, she was able to set up an independent study that allowed her to work at her own pace. She set aside hourly sessions, 8:30 to 9:30 p.m., three times a week, for creativity.

Sylvia's plan did not produce instant success. However, because she had specific goals to work toward, she was able to synchronize all three agendas. Today she is a department store manager, and she sells some of her paintings on the side.

Our purpose is our bottom line for being in the marketplace. When we have the tenacity to stay focused on it, our path may be erratic but it will not be meaningless. We will make the right choices needed to take aim in a specific direction with true singleness of purpose, and refuse to get bogged down in the difficulties that will inevitably come along. Juggling multiple roles, handling competition, or compensating for a sluggish economy may hinder us, but they won't stop us from making a worthwhile contribution.

FEEDBACK: OUR SCORING SYSTEM

Feedback is an important part of staying on track. Imagine being given a job to do, but no one ever tells you if you're doing it right. You have no idea how much progress you're making, and you get no reinforcement for the tasks you do well along the way. Yet you're still expected to keep at it. That would be a pretty tough assignment!

Yet this is what it's like when we make our way through life without any method of evaluating how we're doing in those areas of greatest importance to us. The stress of the uncertainties saps our zeal. We wonder if we're really making any difference.

We need our own form of feedback in life. Using MINI Steps to plan for progress gives us as many chances for feedback as there are steps along the way. What we reach are Milestones; what we receive is feedback.

Just like my children could evaluate how far along we were on trips by checking off the milestones we passed, so we can evaluate how far we're progressing toward our visions by observing the Milestones we achieve along the way. Milestones give us reference points for comparing projected performance against present performance. Let's say a real estate agent's goal is to make the million dollar club. She sets Milestones in hundred thousand dollar increments. Each sale gives her feedback; each Milestone she reaches helps propel her toward the next one, and ultimately toward her overall goal.

Feedback fuels our forward movement by igniting our passion and refreshing our vision. It propels us through an array of opportunities in our career without letting us get too far off-course with other agendas. By giving us new information and insights, it helps us adjust our vision and set our Milestones with greater wisdom and perception. Feedback gives us our score, but it also indicates to us what needs correcting.

To make use of the natural feedback in a MINI Steps plan, highlight each Milestone you've put on your calendar as you accomplish it. This will give you instant feedback.

At the end of each month when you take time for evaluation,

look at all the Milestones you accomplished and ask yourself, "What did I do *right* here?" Look at any you didn't accomplish and ask yourself, "What kept me from achieving my objective?" As you think through these questions, you may notice recurring patterns. Reinforce the ones that are successful, and work on the ones that are hindering your progress.

Another way to keep score is by maintaining frequent entries in a personal journal. Keep these entries brief but precise: "I made a big sale today, which gets me $100 closer to buying my new car." This type of personal feedback will build your confidence by showing you how you're working toward your vision.

ONE STEP AT A TIME

The beauty of MINI Steps is that we're freed from the anxiety of thinking we need all the answers to what's going to happen in the future. We don't have to know every bend along the path ahead—just the next few steps. Instead of worrying about the outcome tomorrow, we can focus on the choices we make today.

MINI Steps start with anticipating change and preparing ourselves to respond to it. In order to take advantage of opportunities, we need to recognize them when they come along but also be informed enough to judge the value of acting on them. We should view opportunity as a frequent visitor, not a fly-by-nighter that may never return. This attitude allows us to think big but take small steps. Like the golfer who moves from tee to tee, playing one shot at a time, we set our direction from Milestone to Milestone.

The story is told of the runner who was observed talking to herself throughout the last stage of the race. After she crossed the finish line, an interviewer asked her what she had been saying. "I was so tired," she said, "that I just kept praying, 'Lord, You pick 'em up, and I'll put 'em down.'" As we move forward in fulfilling our purpose, we can trust God to give us the strength and direction for our next step.

Sometimes we can feel overwhelmed simply because we're not organized. A MINI Step plan will reduce the chaos by enabling us to synchronize all that we want to do. If we're trying to do too much, planning will show us that we need to chisel down our do-list. Setting priorities in our various agendas will help show us where to cut.

A plan takes raw components and forges them into a powerful force for moving ahead. We can take the demands and the desires of personal care, relationships, and professional growth and merge them in a plan that will give us a clear sense of direction and progress.

We don't have to sink under the chaos that confuses us and the stress that overwhelms us. When we stop trying to have it all, all at once, and focus on synchronizing instead of balancing our lives, we can take the defeat out of disappointment. As we develop agility, anticipation, and adaptability, our newfound skills will take us to incredible heights of accomplishment.

CHAPTER EIGHT

TRADE SURVIVAL FOR EXCELLENCE

▼▼▼▼▼▼

*The highest reward for a person's toil is not
what they get for it but what they become by it.*[1]

Recently I looked back through my years in the marketplace at what have been the highest rewards of my work. Searching through the chaos of experience, I've found some nuggets of inspiration that have kept me going. They've all been related to moments in which God brought to the forefront of my thinking the desire to perform with excellence.

As I've searched for what it means to be excellent in the marketplace, I've found that the concept of a quality work life is buried beneath the overwhelming chaos of daily survival. We don't live in a *quality* work world; we live in a *quantity* work world. The demands we live with dictate that we live with what is acceptable, rather than excellent.

Men and women are so busy climbing the corporate ladder that they don't realize the rungs they're stepping on are human lives. Making the sale at the right margin matters more than honesty and keeping one's word. The quality of our clothes is more important than the quality of our work. Employers and employees are polarized on either side of a trust gap. Colleagues care more about getting their share than about giving themselves freely for the common good. The not-so-golden rule is "Do unto others before they can do it unto to you."

This sad state of affairs is the norm. But that doesn't mean it's right. Society has begun to realize that the "anything goes" attitude leads to disaster. The business community is deteriorating as quality is declining. We now hear calls for renewing excellence, quality work, personal and corporate integrity.

We don't have to settle for just getting by. We can do more than just survive our stay in the marketplace. We can trade in survival for excellence.

WHAT IS EXCELLENCE?

After the infamous Watergate scandal of Richard Nixon's presidency, the Secretary of the Air Force advocated a return to excellence. He gave this challenge for our performance in the workplace:

> Let each of your actions be of such high quality, purity, and good faith that if the crew from CBS's "Sixty Minutes" program—or Sam Donaldson, or Ralph Nader, or your company's auditor, or your son or daughter—should ask you about it, you can truthfully and cheerfully say, "I'm glad you asked! We're proud of what we are doing, and I'd like nothing better than to share the whole file in this matter with you, and to give you the complete background on our reasoning."[2]

Would you be glad if someone asked about how you perform at work? If your purpose is to be God's woman in God's plan, then people should be asking you what makes you function with such high quality, honesty, and willingness. Your performance should not blend with the norm; your quality should make it stand out. Your excellence should be exceptional. Remember: becoming an exception is a good kind of different. It means doing your best with every opportunity you're given. It means caring what kind of impact your actions have on others.

You can make a difference by trading in survival for excellence. But before you feel discouraged about achieving some high and mighty ideal, consider what "excellence" really is. It's not a standard of performance as much as a combination of character qualities: *integrity*, the firm adherence to values; *credibility*, the credentials that inspire others to trust you; *responsibility* and *dependability*, your willingness to be committed to accomplishment; and *tenacity*, giving yourself wholeheartedly to doing your best.

Excellence is not an achievement, but something we are continuously, and consciously, working toward. It's quality in progress, not perfectionism. Let's take a look at the character qualities that compose the mentality of excellence.

Integrity

If you want to find excellence in the marketplace, start by looking for *integrity*. Integrity springs from a consistency in our character: our actions are in accord with our values.

Integrity keeps us living by Christian values when "everybody else is doing it." It keeps us from rationalizing behavior in ourselves that we condemn in others. It keeps us trustworthy in our attitudes, our words, and our actions. It keeps us from compromise.

We have enough chaos in the world to keep us awake at night without those nagging feelings of guilt because we're doing something we know is wrong. Sometimes, those wrong actions are errors that we can easily correct: letting an associate take the blame for our mistake; fudging on expense reports; taking office supplies for personal use. When our conscience signals that we're violating our integrity, we need to examine the cause and deal with it promptly.

No matter what our expertise, the position we've reached, the possessions we've accumulated — it's all meaningless if we compromise our integrity. Laureen was offered a big promotion, but she knew that in a few months her husband would be transferred and they would be leaving town. The promotion would involve several months of training, so Laureen felt it would be unfair to accept the position short-term, at her company's expense. She told her employer about the future move and declined the offer. Her boss was surprised that she had made this choice, when she could have kept quiet about the transfer.

When asked about her decision Laureen commented, "I sleep well at night." Her employer prized her integrity and worked with her through the relocation to help her find another position.

Integrity allows us to feel good about our achievements because we haven't compromised our beliefs to attain them. It gives us the sense that we're winning the war, even if we lose a battle here and there.

In addition to this internal satisfaction, integrity also sends out an external reflection of excellence. Our tough commitment when others compromise stands out like a light that glows—an attitude of care that puts "what is right" before "what I can get."

Patty and Chris had become friends through working together in the cosmetics section of a large department store. Chris liked Patty but did not want anything to do with her Christian convictions. Patty, realizing Chris's reluctance, didn't push her beliefs but prayed that Chris would develop an interest in hearing more about them.

Through a period of several months, Chris began to notice how different Patty was from everyone else in the department. Patty never left "just a few minutes" early. She didn't deceive customers, even though they all worked on commission. Patty always chose what was right, not what would be to her greatest benefit.

One day while on a break together, Chris finally asked Patty, "Why don't you compromise to get ahead? Everyone else does." Patty took this opportunity to tell Chris about her convictions. This time, Chris was all ears. Patty's integrity had opened the door. It was starting to become contagious.

Sometimes our integrity gets us bad reviews instead of admiring ones. Those whose ethics are questionable will often resent the commitment of others. When others belittle us for our integrity, we can take comfort in knowing that it's better to be singled out for doing what is right than for doing what is wrong.

For God's woman, integrity involves more than just adhering to a code of ethics. It becomes a way of life that flows out of our basic beliefs. We develop integrity as we look beyond do's and don'ts to acquiring the character qualities that emerge as we follow through on God's commands: steadfastness and courage in doing what is right; honesty with self and others; wisdom in setting the right priorities. Integrity rests on this bottom line: "trust and obey, for there's no other way" to reflect Christ in the marketplace.

The marketplace is looking for people with integrity to bridge the trust gap. Women of integrity can be a beacon for others who are seeking direction in the turbulence of the work world.

Credibility

Integrity reflects our character; *credibility* reflects our performance. The better quality our work, the more credible we are. Credibility means that others can rely on us and will respect us. It reflects excellence as it inspires others to believe in us. They can say with confidence, "I trust you to know what you're doing and to do it right."

Many of us can immediately think of people we know in the business community who have credibility. These are the people we would list as references on a job application. They're the people employers depend on for good advice and sound opinions. They've proven themselves over time.

Credibility is earned, not claimed. We earn it through experience, demonstrated skills, and consistency in giving our best. Think of it from a financial standpoint: you gain credibility with a lender by consistently making payments on time. One missed payment has more impact than many timely payments. We earn credibility by being diligent and faithful with every task we are given.

Attaining credibility doesn't require a perfect record, unblemished by failure. We reach it when our performance record is recognized by those around us even when we do have setbacks.

Suzanne was the assistant manager of a large mall. The

manager's position had just opened up, but she figured her young age would disqualify her from consideration. However, through the credibility she had earned through innovative promotions, supervisory leadership, and following through when others failed to do so, she had gained a solid reputation. When the decision was made for a new manager, age was not a factor. Suzanne's credibility based on jobs well done gave her an edge over the other candidates.

Responsibility and Dependability

Responsibility is willingness to make a commitment. *Dependability* is following through on that commitment. This pair of character traits is a major component of excellence.

Responsible people are willing to do what needs to be done even when "it's not their department." They make a stronger, more active commitment to the task and its outcome. Work can be delegated, but responsibility for it must be assumed.

Developing a responsible character is a benefit—it places us in a self-motivational process that keeps us moving forward even against obstacles. We don't get sidetracked blaming others, but forge ahead in search of the best way to get the job done right.

Here is where dependability comes in. It builds on responsibility by making the necessary adjustments—whether in schedules, strategies, or attitudes—to meet the commitments we've made. Dependable people meet the requests of those responsible for them and meet the needs of those for whom they're responsible.

Beth went to work for a progressive company as a sales associate. She demonstrated a willingness to assume responsibility for whatever needed to be done. She quickly became the person everyone depended on in the clutch. She was there when she was supposed to be, and even beyond, when necessary. Her marketplace excellence made her a valuable member of the company.

Beth's superior performance paid dividends when she acted on her desire to attend college. Because her employer knew she was willing to accept responsibility and could be depended on to finish her work, they supported her efforts at furthering her education.

It's amazing how many people in the marketplace miss opportunities because they don't assume responsibility or demonstrate dependability. When we're willing to act before being asked, we learn far more than sitting around waiting for someone to tell us what to do. Our initiative in showing interest and ability can put us first in line when opportunities come along. And they can turn "just a job" into a stimulating and stretching experience.

Tenacity

The glue that holds our excellence together is *tenacity*. It's persistence in maintaining high standards; a commitment to hang in there and give it our best no matter what.

Tenacious people have the guts to do what it takes, even when it seems to take more than they can give. Performing with excellence isn't a guarantee that everything is always going to turn out right. Often we're faced with a set of circumstances in which very few variables are under our control. To stay committed to excellence under these conditions requires tenacity. It keeps us going to the rhythm of *"Don't quit."*

This poem has helped me keep smiling when I've been accountable for circumstances beyond anyone's control:

> When things go wrong, as they sometimes will,
> When the road you're trudging seems all up hill,
> When the funds are low, and the debts are high,
> And you want to smile, but you have to sigh,
> When care is pressing you down a bit,
> Rest if you must, but don't you quit.[3]

Annette joined a marketing communications company in its start-up stage. Her partner was involved in several outside projects, so the burden fell on Annette's shoulders to assume responsibility for making sure the business moved forward. The learning curve was so steep that Annette could easily have compromised quality under pressure for quantity. But she stuck to her commitment to excellence even in the face of multiple deadlines pressing in on her. Her tenacity won her a reputation among her clients for quality service.

THE PROCESS OF EXCELLENCE

Just because you get a car up to speed at sixty miles per hour doesn't mean you can let up on the gas. If you don't keep the fuel flowing, the vehicle will slow down to a stop.

The same is true in our cultivation of excellence. We can't rest on our laurels or past experience. We must keep striving. I defined excellence earlier as quality in progress, not a perfectionistic achievement. A commitment to excellence means *a commitment to the process of becoming our best.*

Futurist Alvin Toffler suggests that the information age presents liabilities not so much for those who can't read and write as for those who are not teachable.

The attitude of teachability, or the mindset of the learner, is a crucial factor in maintaining a quality work life. The willingness to learn and relearn is a key part of making progress in excellence. Here are five steps to becoming a lifelong learner:

1. *Learn by observing.* Be on the alert to notice what is going on around you. Instead of resting on what you know, continually ask yourself, *What don't I understand, and how can I learn it?*

2. *Stay flexible.* Trade in the mindset, "but we've always done it this way" for an attitude of expectation and adaptability. Our world is constantly changing—computers that were new yesterday are obsolete today. Manufacturers know about the critical need for continual upgrading in order to compete. We must maintain a position of flexibility in order to meet new challenges with a response of excellence.

3. *Be a good listener.* The true learner is always open to acquiring advice and information from those around her. Practice listening to what others are saying—not to respond, but to understand and absorb. Soak in all the information you can acquire.

4. *Learn from followers as well as leaders.* In our cultural preoccupation with authority and position, we often forget how much

we can learn from those who work for us or who are new on the team. They have strengths that we don't. And often their position as "followers" gives them insight and perspective that we don't have. Don't limit your range of vision to people who are high-profile.

5. *Fail forward.* Failures don't have to be setbacks. When you learn from mistakes, failures can put you ahead. Use them as stepping stones to insights you can put to use in the future.

OUR SOURCE OF EXCELLENCE

The decision to pursue excellence is up to us. But let's not forget that the process of excellence is the process of becoming who God created us to be. The source of the character qualities that define excellence is not some inner pool of resources that we dredge up through force of will, but the living stream of God's grace flowing through us.

It's our responsibility, however, to draw from this stream in order to maintain excellence in the marketplace. This accountability is our bottom line: we are answerable for the method of our performance, the motives for our actions, and the demonstration of our commitment.

As God's women in God's plan, we must stand up and be counted among those who pursue excellence. The buck stops with us.

Our true goal in pursuing excellence is not to receive recognition for our performance, however. Ultimately, it is to please God—which gives us great freedom from cultural stereotypes of excellence. We have a model of this kind of living in those who belonged to the early church. In his book *Birthright*, David Needham points out five elements that characterized these early believers' lives of excellence:[4]

1. *They knew who they were and why they were alive.* Their identity was based on the foundation of a solid awareness of the character of God and the final authority of His written Word.

2. *They knew that holiness was not passively acquired.* It required the active participation of their individual will.

3. *They knew that the lordship of Christ was not optional.* They had an accurate understanding of the true authority structure of this world.

4. *They knew the Holy Spirit's presence as an experienced reality.* These individuals were renewed by the daily reality of God's empowering love and strength.

5. *They perceived the individual Christian not as an isolated pilgrim, but as part of a Body that would not function apart from love.* They saw their relationships with one another as a crucial part of the excellence they were called to.

These elements can characterize our lives when we grasp the truth that excellence in the marketplace begins with who we are becoming in God's plan. This truth frees us to give quality service as we place our actions in God's hands. We're not stuck in a holding pattern until something better comes along. Our purpose is rooted in a reality that transcends the fluctuating circumstances of the workplace.

STAYING ON TRACK

For me, pursuing excellence always comes down to being God's woman in God's plan—unconditionally.

But this pursuit can seem like a tall order when we face the reality that there's no guarantee our career will take the route we want it to. When we're caught up in anxiety about the future, there's little room for thinking about our performance other than how it's going to affect us. When our carefully-aimed plans fall wide of the target, the desire for excellence quickly gives way to envy or resentment. How do we stay on track when there are so many temptations to deter us?

I think it's based on one important issue: *trusting God.* If we don't believe that God is trustworthy, then we won't have the confidence to stay on track in the process of excellence. We'll put conditions on our performance that will ultimately lead to compromise and confusion—right back into chaos.

We must choose to believe God is trustworthy, then we can begin to experience His trustworthiness when circumstances take an unexpected turn. This experience gives us a growing foundation from which we choose to trust Him again in the future.

I discovered that trusting God was critical in my ability to counteract the overwhelming presence of market competition. My challenge was to use competition to keep me on my toes (and my knees!) rather than allowing it to control my business. When I learned to trust God in this part of the business, I developed the conviction that if our business gave quality service, used good business practices, and functioned according to biblical principles, we would get all the business we were supposed to have. Whatever business we didn't get wasn't ours to be had.

This conviction was not a resignation to the attitude, "whatever will be, will be." It was based on the thought process, "I've done my job with excellence. That's my responsibility. Now it's up to God, because I can't do anything more." I was not using God in hopes that He would make the business succeed; I was making myself willing to be used by Him.

Once we develop a lifestyle of trusting God, we begin to develop *trustworthiness*. As we're anchored in His purpose, our lives will reflect a level of excellence that others will notice. They will see that we choose to do what is right regardless of the conditions.

Excellence in the marketplace should be a priority for Christian working women. We should have a reputation for being trustworthy. To keep foremost in my mind the qualities to be a trustworthy businesswoman, I think about those areas in which people should be able to say to me, "I Trust You." I've developed what I call an "I-T-Y" mindset for excellence. I visualize others saying to me, "I trust you to have integrity and tenacity. To display credibility, dependability, responsibility, and teachability."

Pursuing excellence means applying these characteristics in meeting challenges—whether in business strategies or in the lives of people. As we stay on track in striving to be women of excellence in the marketplace, we will set an example for others. It's been said that "people are more persuaded by the depth of our commitment to excellence than by the height of our logic." Trading in survival for excellence means being exceptional.

GOING THE EXTRA MILE

During the reign of the Roman Empire, soldiers were legally permitted to conscript boys to carry their heavy packs — but only for a maximum distance of one mile.

One day a young boy tried to run away when a soldier commanded him to carry his pack. The boy was caught and returned to the soldier, who again commanded the boy to come pick up his pack. The boy approached, cringing in fear of a whipping for his attempted refusal. To his surprise, the soldier simply handed him the pack and commented, "Come with me."

The two trudged along the rugged road in silence. When they reached the end of the mile, the soldier gave the boy permission to leave. But the boy reshouldered the pack and willingly carried it a second mile. The soldier spoke to the boy this time, sharing stories about marvelous things the boy had never seen.

When the boy was asked why he went the extra mile he responded, "I discovered an important secret. The first mile is duty. When you go the second mile you begin to experience the rewards."

We've been talking in this chapter about giving. But excellence has its own rewards. It's possible that you were forced to enter the marketplace. Or, if you chose your career course with excitement and enthusiasm, you may have found that the going is often rough. Perhaps at this stage it's more duty than reward. However, by becoming God's woman in God's plan through your commitment to excellence in the marketplace, you can experience the joy of "walking the extra mile."

Decide that you will be the exception to the struggle for survival. You may be surprised to find that you will fill your own needs as well as meeting those of others. As you focus on giving, you will find yourself receiving the joy of God's presence in the midst of chaotic conditions.

In the next section of this book we'll be exploring what the journey of work is all about — becoming a beacon of influence. Your walk through the marketplace is God's masterpiece on exhibit. Sign it with excellence.

PART FOUR

BECOMING A BEACON IN THE MARKETPLACE

*Remembering What the Journey
Is All About*

▼▼▼▼▼▼

CHAPTER NINE

YOU CAN INFLUENCE OTHERS THROUGH C.E.O. LEADERSHIP

▼▼▼▼▼▼

*Real leaders are ordinary people
with extraordinary determination who
ignite in others a passion of purpose.*

At first glance you might think Janelle was just another one of the women in the office. She didn't design her appearance to be attention-grabbing, yet the vivacious way she projected herself would always make others take a second look. She wasn't an ambitious climber, but simply a woman who worked in order to care for her family's needs.

Janelle wasn't in a position of authority, but when it came time to present the annual leadership award that the staff voted on, Janelle's name was called.

What made Janelle a leader? *She had a way of recognizing potential in the people she worked with — and encouraging them to develop it.* Janelle had a sensitivity that enabled her to accept others without judging them, all the while helping them to improve and move forward.

Janelle always gave her best, without ever using others to make herself look good. She never claimed to have all the answers, but she had a knack for finding out who was the right resource. The management depended on her as the glue that held the office team together through her peacemaking skills and her role as a catalyst in sparking momentum to complete projects.

Progress occurred when Janelle was around because everyone wanted to keep up with her. Her enthusiasm opened the eyes of others to see the vision for themselves or the team. She was truly a beacon in the marketplace, illuminating good paths for others to take. She made an impact wherever she went.

I think all of us want to have a positive influence on people. Deep down, we hope that the world will be different in a better way, that others' lives will be better off, because we have lived.

I'm going to talk about a particular kind of leadership. Like Janelle's, it's not limited to position or personality. I call it "C.E.O. Leadership." The initials refer not to "Chief Executive Officer" but to *Catalyst Empowering Others*. I firmly believe that the heart of true leadership is not directing other people's behavior, but empowering them to direct themselves.

A NEW DEFINITION OF LEADERSHIP

There's a saying that leaders are born, not made. But it's not true. People become leaders when they develop qualities that empower others to reach their potential. I like to put it this way: *leaders are cultivated, not delegated.*

Our ability to lead increases with our ability to make personal connections with others. The process of influence occurs like osmosis: others assimilate what they observe in the example we set. We rub off on them.

Many of us have an outdated definition of leadership. We think of leaders as only those people who are in a position of authority—those who command, direct, impose, bring along, enforce. We need to switch over to the new definition: *a leader is a catalyst who empowers others.* This is a more flexible understanding, which applies in any kind of context and has more enduring results than the narrow and rigid traditional definition.

This new kind of leader acts as a spark to ignite in others the desire to take action. A C.E.O. Leader kindles the process of becoming. Janelle, whose leadership was not a mandated position but the effect of her influence on others' actions, is a good example of authentic leadership: not making people do what we want them to do, but *motivating them to want to do what they should be doing.*

With this new definition of leadership comes a new understanding of power. Power is no longer a tool to enforce authority: for reward — "you'll get more if you do what I want you to do"; for punishment — "you'll be sorry if you don't"; for pulling rank — "just do it because I said so." Instead, *power is the influence on others that arises from who we are.* It's based on factors like credibility (respect earned by our accomplishments) and charisma (the draw we exert on others based on their confidence in our integrity and in our care for them).

Influence is an awesome power. We all have the power to influence others, positively or negatively. In order for us to have the right kind of influence, we need to be responsible and accountable in how we use that power. When we use power in the right way, we don't give away our strength; we multiply potential.

A LEADER FOR ALL SEASONS

C.E.O. Leadership can take place anytime, anywhere. It begins with a deep sense of awareness that our actions affect those around us. It develops as we change our mindset from "Where is this going to get me?" to "Where am I leading others?"

We're in a position to lead others wherever our lives touch other lives. I call this the "influence zone." It occurs in our family, our network of relationships, our workplace. We step outside this influence zone when we start looking at ourselves as the solution to others' needs — a recipe for unhealthy relationships and burnout. When we work within the influence zone, we recognize that we have impact in all of our agendas as our influence becomes a factoring agent in others' decisions.

With the massive entrance of women into the work force in recent decades has come a need for front runners. The business community is searching for strong leadership among women. Think of the potential for good, in human lives as well as business growth, if working women would begin to see themselves as catalysts empowering others. All those beacons could shed a lot of light!

Grasping the truth of our unbounded ability to have an impact can help us get through those times when taxing demands make us feel drained instead of empowered. So often when we're surrounded by the complaining, the competitiveness, the contradictory behavior, we're tempted to throw in the towel and exclaim, "What's the use?" The Apostle Paul's words can help us here, as he encourages us to see beyond the chaos to our purpose:

> Do everything without complaining or arguing, so that you may become blameless and pure, children of God without fault in a crooked and depraved generation, in which you shine like stars in the universe.[1]

There comes a time when we must make a choice to be more than a gatekeeper, guarding our positions and our relationships as we clutch to ourselves what we've acquired. We have the chance to become a pacesetter in all our spheres of influence—a woman in the process of becoming more like the Master, who influences others to follow Him as she shows them what they can become.

SPREADING THE INFLUENCE

Earlier in this book I spoke of how we're driven by our purpose and drawn by our vision. This is essential for leadership. Before we can influence others effectively, we must know who we are and where we are leading.

There's no set formula for how to develop leadership capabilities. We bring to the table our assets as well as our liabilities and put them to use as best we can in service to others, meeting their needs and encouraging their potential.

In their book *Reinventing the Corporation*, John Naisbitt and Patricia Aburdene comment, "Women can transform the workplace by expressing, not giving up, their personal values."[2] We don't need to fit a certain profile to become catalysts; we need to use who we are as leverage to move others forward. As we learn all we can and seek to professionalize our innate strengths — such as the ability to share openly, or sensitivity to others — we will develop our natural leadership abilities along the way.

I've referred to transferring skills from one agenda to another, and this applies to leadership traits as well. For example, I learned to look at interruptions from my children as teaching experiences, and this has helped me in training people in the marketplace.

Our traits and learned skills can be opportunities or liabilities, depending upon how we apply them. Here is where we especially need to be aware of the expectations we harbor, for ourselves and those we influence. A key factor in developing realistic expectations, and not getting tripped up by unrealistic expectations, is knowing our strengths and weaknesses.

I want to look at the opportunities and liabilities of three characteristics that women bring to the marketplace: nurturing capacity, emotional sensitivity, and relational orientation. These are sometimes perceived as weaknesses in women leaders, but they can also be strengths. Like everything else, character traits have their flip side. Awareness of who we are and what our purpose is has a lot to do with which side we're on.

Our influence on others increases as we guard against the potential pitfalls of our weaknesses and build on our strengths. We may never have the reach of leaders such as Corrie Ten Boom or Abraham Lincoln, but we can match their depth of influence by developing the same qualities and skills for empowering others that they possessed.

OPPORTUNITIES AND LIABILITIES

There's been some debate about whether the characteristics of nurturing, emotional sensitivity, and relational ability are unique to women. Generally, they show up as overall tendencies. In some cases, the reason may be generational rather than gender-related: until recent decades women were usually the care-givers and men the providers. As these roles cross over and interact, the tendencies may shift according to individual personality rather than gender.

However, I think these three traits are prominent factors in the ability of women to empower others. Let's look at how they can contribute to or undermine leadership development.

Nurturing Capacity

Women are especially geared toward nurturing. This can be a powerful tool for empowering others, but it can also become an excuse for catering to or controlling them.

The nurturing tendency is a liability when it's not tempered with leadership skills. An example of this flip side occurred in an organization that became concerned over a branch manager who was not making the sales calls she was responsible for. After extensive effort to research the cause they discovered that the branch manager was letting her nurturing instincts inappropriately direct her actions.

The scenario went something like this: when the branch manager would begin to leave the office to make her calls, an associate would invariably express anxiety over how to handle problems that might arise while she was gone. Instead of empowering her associates to make the necessary adjustments to her absences, the manager stayed at the office. She allowed her behavior to be dictated by her fear of rejection on the sales calls and her desire to nurture her associates, which made her feel needed.

The same pattern can occur in the domains of home or relationships. All too often, we use the desire to nurture as a means to forming a dependency, rather than as a means of furthering the development of other people and thus fostering their independence.

On the other hand, our innate desire to care for others and help them grow and develop presents a great opportunity for becoming a catalyst in their lives. When we care instead of cater or control, we can make a major investment in someone else's life—whether that someone is a child, a spouse, a parent, a colleague, or a friend.

Charlene, a branch manager at the same organization I just

mentioned, illustrated how nurturing capacity can be a strength. She recognized the detrimental effect of her employees' assumption that they were unable to handle problems. Instead of trying to solve their problems for them, she began working with them to build confidence in their abilities. She took specific steps to reinforce their successes in handling situations and to build confidence in her own salesmanship.

The benefits of Charlene's leadership to the organization were at least twofold: first, there was a ten percent increase in new customers; second, Charlene had demonstrated to her employees that she cared about their feelings, but she used that caring to develop their abilities rather than cater to their dependence.

There are many other examples of how the desire to nurture is a key part of leadership influence. Consider these: the mother who sees problems as possibilities and can discern when to hold on and when to let go; the friend who knows when to encourage and when to confront; the office associate who invests her interest and energy in the performance and well-being of those around her.

Emotional Sensitivity
Women have often been accused of being "too emotional." Sometimes this is simply inaccurate, and a reaction based on unfair stereotypes. After all, men have emotions too, and both women and men fall into the "too emotional" category at times.

But the general tendency is that women often display greater emotional sensitivity than men. The liability here is *emotionalism*, which means allowing our emotions to direct our behavior inappropriately.

Emotionalism can crop up from many different seeds: if hormones aren't enough to send us into tailspins, then not far away lies the chaos of multiple roles that we're supposed to live in simultaneously. Like it or not, these factors come with the territory. It's not a simple task to lead with feelings instead of allowing our feelings to lead us.

I recently came down with a classic case of emotionalism in a situation that caught me off-guard. What surprised me was not just the situation, but even more, my response to it. A combination of unmet expectations, exhaustion, and frustration had conspired to set up the dry tinder to which my emotions touched the match.

After it was all over and done with, I felt drained and defeated. For years I had restrained myself and been "the professional." Now I had become "the emotional woman." Instead of controlling my emotions, they had controlled my behavior. I could have handled the situation differently had I waited to react until I wasn't so tired, taken my personal expectations into consideration, and realized that part of my frustration was misdirected. Instead of using my emotional sensitivity to help me form the right response, I had let it sabotage my response in this encounter.

Some areas in which we might need to be especially alert to the pitfalls of emotional sensitivity include the following: taking action when it can be taken, but changing course when circumstances are out of our control; reacting to moments of success with satisfaction for milestones achieved rather than with childish exhilaration; handling conflicts constructively without creating a crisis environment.

The opportunity to become a catalyst through emotional sensitivity requires developing composure in the midst of chaos. I like the term "stability in action." When we avoid taking our mood swings into the marketplace and practice self-control, we can use our feelings as assets. Empathy with others—feeling as they feel—can strengthen the bonds of our relationships.

Communicating our emotional sensitivity can be an effective leadership tool. Two factors are especially important here: listening and clarifying. We should avoid assuming that we know what others are feeling, and make a conscious effort to learn their true thoughts, feeling, visions—what motivates them. Nor should we expect others to read our thoughts or feelings, which is frustrating for both parties.

When emotions threaten to take the bit and run with it, listening and clarifying can be helpful controls. Making the extra effort to understand another's point of view and become aware of what is going on inside us can help us cling to the passion of purpose instead of being swept up in the passion of pressure and panic.

Miscommunications happen daily in the marketplace. A manager makes a seemingly simple statement that a usually compatible associate takes the wrong way. Why? Often because of the emotions of the moment. Emotions can gather up many combinations of perceptions, tones, words, inferences, and past events, and create chaos with them.

This is why developing strong communication skills to guide emotional sensitivity is so important for leadership. A good place to start is with the many excellent books currently available that suggest how to corral emotions and use them as leverage — instead of letting them corrupt our ability to influence others by leading us into emotionalism.

Relational Orientation
Another way to define leadership is to call it *a style of interaction in relationships*. This helps take it out of the realm of authority and into the realm of influence. We can look at C.E.O. Leadership as a way of functioning in our relationships.

Women tend to be oriented toward relationships rather than tasks. The up side is that we form bonds easily; we value being there when someone needs an anchor or an igniter. The down side is that we can lose perspective on when those bonds are healthy and when they're unhealthy.

I think the greatest liability of our relational orientation is that sometimes we don't know when too much is too much. We can get to a point of believing we're all things to all people.

This "be everything to everybody" complex sometimes takes the form of thinking that we know what is best for other people. Because we think we have all the answers, we justify our manipulation of people and circumstances to create what we want to happen.

Leadership does not give us ownership. We have neither the right nor the perception to mastermind other people's careers, personal growth, or thoughts.

The challenge in avoiding this liability is to work on accepting people and circumstances, staying focused on the issue confronting us instead of on the individual or our personal interest. Here I've found it helpful to remember the "serenity prayer": "God grant me the serenity to accept the things I cannot change, the courage to change the things I can, and the wisdom to know the difference."

During my bleakest days of early adulthood, I drew strength from this prayer, which was engraved on a charm bracelet I often wore. Every time I began to react to the emotions of the moment, to dwell on the effects rather than the potential, this prayer reminded me that my actions in the marketplace and in personal circumstances needed to be driven by purpose, not people. I needed to base my choices on what *I* could do, not on what I could make others do.

Our relational orientation also presents us with great opportunities for influencing others. There are many of them, but I will single out two, which are especially relevant to working women: *mentoring* and *networking*.

My close friend Peg Haddad was a mentor to me. She was an experienced and trusted counselor, teacher, tutor, and coach. I think each of us has someone like Peg in our lives. Although we may not call them a "mentor," they have mentored us: a grandparent or parent, a friend, a teacher, a co-worker, even a sibling. Simply stated, mentors are people who through their experience, wisdom, and encouragement kindled our vision and growth along the way.

The word *mentor* may have ascended to popularity recently, but the concept has been around forever. My best friend's mother, whom I affectionately called Aunt Irene, taught me that mentoring roles should be passed on. Back in the mid-fifties she would pull up to the door of our small home in Jacksonville, Florida, and take me to church on days when the weather didn't permit me to walk.

One day I asked her, "What can I ever do to repay you for all you've done for me?"

"Don't worry about paying me back," she replied. "Just

always be aware of the needs of others and be looking for how you can help them." This is an important part of mentoring: not pay-back, but pass-it-on.

Mentorship has become a recognized topic in the marketplace today. Changes in society have women in the work force looking for experienced advisers who can help them along their career path. Unfortunately, there is a shortage of role models—women who merge their professionalism and their relationships with care.

The most effective mentor is not the woman who is positioned to open the right doors, but the woman who can help others develop and learn how to open their own doors. The purpose in this relationship should be growth in the right direction, not a shortcut to professional success.

Liz found herself going back to school to get a teaching certificate after working closely with one of her children's teachers. During their interaction, the teacher had pointed out characteristics in Liz that were natural assets in the teaching profession. She helped Liz put together a plan that would allow Liz to attend college part-time in preparation for entering the work force by the time her children were old enough.

"People seldom improve when they have no other model but themselves to copy," it's been said. Mentors are valuable resources for working women.

Another resource rooted in women's relational orientation is *networking*: a professionalized way for groups of women to share insights and confront challenges based on their experience.

Here again women seem to have a natural affinity that is less common among men. Perhaps our relative ease in sharing is in part a result of socialization: We were taught it's okay to say "help," but our male counterparts were constrained by the warning to "act like a man." Whatever the underlying reasons, networking provides a valuable opportunity for women to spread their influence.

Networking groups offer the chance to listen to other women and become aware of their circumstances and needs. They're an ideal channel for giving and receiving support. When we've been care-giving too long and are slow to drop our guard for care-taking, network groups give us a safe place. This is especially important for women who have developed a strong defense mechanism under society's pressure not to show "weakness."

Clarissa, a personnel manager, found herself stymied on a personal problem. She was reluctant to ask for help from her colleagues, since she wanted to maintain her reputation as the answer person. She finally turned to her roommates, Paula and Sarah, for help in gaining insights toward a solution.

It turned out that Paula had already been through a similar situation and had developed a way of turning an obstacle into an opportunity. The three women then started a networking group to discuss developing strengths and dealing with emotional marketplace issues. This strategy empowered them to increase their effectiveness and eliminate the sense of being alone in facing challenges.

For many women in the marketplace, joining a personal networking group has provided an uplifting and constructive source of encouragement, insight, information, feedback on ideas and implementation, help in working through conflicts, and shared experience. A few hours once a month can make a big difference.

Networking groups function most effectively when they're composed of women who face the same issues on a daily basis — managers with managers, teachers with teachers, etc. I've found that pre-planned agendas, a facilitator, and an agreement to hold discussions (never gossip sessions) in strictest confidence maximize the group's contribution.

BECOMING A C.E.O. LEADER

You've seen those people who ignite a spark of interest in others — a secretary, a manager, a boss — because they have a passion for what they do. Their enthusiasm invites others to connect with their momentum.

What is it that gives these individuals their capacity to empower others? *They understand what they are best equipped to do, and they put their potential to maximum use.* Purposefully turning everyday tasks into opportunities, they meet conflicts and confrontations with a consistent confidence. Watching for opportunities that knock ever so softly, they turn them into investments in the future—for themselves and others.

Contagiousness of purpose is what creates true leaders. A leader who is a catalyst empowering others communicates a vision that others want to take hold of—or inspires others to create and pursue their own vision.

How do we get on the road to becoming a C.E.O. Leader? Most importantly, by opening ourselves to how God wants to use us to influence others. Recently I was going to work on one of those days when I knew I would need extra strength and wisdom as well as double the hours I had. Driving down the road I whispered, "God, please be with me. I need You today!"

All of a sudden an overwhelming realization hit me as I sensed God whispering back, "What about me? I need you today too!" How seldom we stop to grasp the awesome thought that God needs us too. We feel so insignificant most of the time that we lose sight of how important a purpose God has for us. He needs us to be His beacon in the marketplace, to shed light on others' paths. What a privilege this responsibility is!

Once we're on the road to this kind of influence, the "how" of our journey is following the customized road plan God has mapped out for us. As we seek to follow His leading day by day, we will fill the niche of the particular influence zone in which God has placed us.

When I was first asked what it was like to be CEO of one of America's fastest growing companies, I responded, "I'm sure no Lee Iacocca." I felt uncomfortable with the title "Chief Executive Officer" because although I was performing the same tasks as Mr. Iacocca, it was on a much smaller scale.

But the question got me thinking about the privilege of being in a position to influence others. I realized that I was a CEO for a purpose: to be a Catalyst Empowering Others. This is a position given to me by God. When I accept this position, I gain a new sense of what I'm really trying to accomplish in all that I do.

My goal of having a positive impact in the marketplace takes on a deeper significance. I can go beyond worrying about my position in the marketplace to a concern for my position in the lives of those around me.

If you want to read about the life of an excellent role model for C.E.O. Leadership, consult the Gospel narratives in the New Testament. I think Jesus was the perfect C.E.O. He was prepared to meet the needs of those He was accountable for. He walked where they walked, leading them along rather than pushing them by pressure. For those who were open to His leadership, He cared rather than condemned. He gave to them without strings attached, without a hidden agenda of self-interest.

Jesus invested years of time, energy, and care in training His disciples. He taught them the principles upon which to base their future; He demonstrated His methods of movement through the marketplace, igniting in them the same passion of purpose; He empowered them to move forward on their own when the time would come.

Because Christ offers to live His life in us, we all have the potential to be influential leaders. It may not happen in a structured or formalized context, but it will occur when we pursue a vision and prepare ourselves to respond effectively within an ever-changing environment. No matter what kind of circumstances we're in, someone is always looking to us to set a pattern. We can show the way to purposeful living.

To become God's woman in God's plan, we must be a catalyst for change—from the inside out. This occurs as we develop a commitment to the truth of God's Word; ask for the wisdom God promises He will provide; let our method of ministry in the marketplace ignite in others a passion of purpose; seek to empower others to follow the call of their own God-given plan.

I urge you to be a dynamic leader. Let your passion of purpose inspire others to see beyond chaos to the meaning in chaotic conditions. You'll find that becoming a C.E.O. is not acquiring a title—it's gaining an identity. It's not leverage for advancement, but leverage for living.

CHAPTER TEN

SUCCESS –
HITTING THE RIGHT
TARGETS

Success is a journey,
not a destination.

Renee was an accomplished young executive. One day I asked her if she considered herself successful.

"I'm considered very successful," she responded emphatically. "I'm the vice president of my company and next in line to become president. I'm on several boards of directors and have received a vast number of awards and recognitions. My neighborhood spells success by any standards. What do *you* think?"

I had shocked Renee with my question. She simply assumed that everyone viewed her as successful, and indeed we did. But Renee hadn't quite heard my question: I had asked her if *she* considered herself successful – not if others did. As convincingly as she answered me, I sensed an element of doubt in her response. So I turned her question back around to her again.

"More importantly than what I think," I said, looking at her, "what do *you* think?"

At this she dropped her gaze and said quietly, "I don't know. I don't *feel* successful. The world says I'm a success, but success should make you feel good. On the inside, I wonder, *If I'm so successful then why do I have so many problems?* My husband is constantly threatened by my position, yet he wants me to work.

My boss depends upon me, but he never thinks enough is enough. I keep going so I can be a success — at least in the eyes of others — but I'm always wondering, *When am I going to feel good about this?"*

Renee's ambivalence is just a glimpse of a much larger picture in today's marketplace. We've lost touch with the real meaning of success. The "ultimate" rewards of recognition and possessions don't deliver on their promise of ultimate satisfaction. The effort to earn them exacts a cost that we find out only later was too steep. Our confidence in the people who are supposedly successful declines as their lives seem to collapse from pressures within and without. We can't count on them anymore to hold up the definition.

What does it mean to be "successful"? What should we be aiming for as the mark of achieving "success" in our careers?

I believe that what working women are *really* searching for is not the immediate gratification of "success," but rather those accomplishments that have lasting significance. We want credibility, not applause. Deep down we want to feed our soul, not our image.

Women are tired of trying to hit targets that others set up for them. Many of us know what it's like to step into the trap of living according to other people's expectations. It's no consolation that the goals belong to someone else when we're flooded with guilt over failing in our agendas. We flinch under the tyranny of success as defined by acceptance — we measure success by how well we're accepted by others, and we measure that acceptance by how well we think we can live up to their expectations. It becomes a vicious circle.

We need a new definition of success. We need a new understanding that gets rid of empty stereotypes and replaces them with a multi-faceted concept that accounts for individual differences and reaches down to the level of what truly satisfies us.

This new understanding must define success in terms of what is important to *me* as well as what is important to those whose lives are affected by *me*. If we're driven by the opinions and standards of others, we're dooming ourselves to total frustration. And if we narrow our vision only to what matters to *me*, we're confining ourselves to self-centered living and a negative impact on those around us.

Think for a minute about what mental images come to your mind when you hear the word "success." The corner office with big windows, fine oak furniture, and tastefully arranged plants? The long-awaited chat with your boss about your glowing future with the company? Becoming a well-known and highly-respected member of a professional peer group? Model children who are a credit to their parents?

Many of us picture success in terms like these because we think of success as recognition for accomplishment. But it doesn't occur only after the fact, as a passive state conferred on us. *Success is an active process of accomplishments along the way.*

This means that we can't pin success down to that point when we cross over the line of having "arrived." I can't describe to you what success is, because actually it's in the eye of the beholder. Its definition changes according to age, conditions, and quests. When I was a year old, I probably thought learning to walk was the greatest success of my life. There's a good chance that by three I was fearing failure because I couldn't walk as fast as my big brother. Success is relative.

Doris and Diane roomed together in college. Upon graduation, both secured positions in corporate America.

Doris married her high school sweetheart and decided to slow down her career in order to make family her top priority. She took a position that was not very demanding, yet paid her enough to supplement the family income. This gave her time for family without the pressure of the extra responsibilities required for advancement.

Diane accepted a position that placed her on the climb up the corporate ladder. She threw her energies into innovative changes within the company that won her successive promotions.

Who became successful? Each of them did, for two reasons. First, *they accomplished what they wanted to do according to their priorities.* Doris put family first; Diane, career. Second, *they had a beneficial impact on the people they were involved with.* Doris set an example in managing the working mom position by meeting her family's needs for her presence and support while fulfilling her obligations to her employer. Diane cut new paths for career women to follow through the marketplace. Their different plans created different conditions for their success. The targets they hit were different, but for Doris and Diane they were *the right targets*.

SUCCESS IN THREE DIMENSIONS

The tendency to get caught up in our national obsession with success often obscures our vision of what we truly want to achieve. In order to get a clear picture of what it means to be "successful," we need to view success in its three dimensions: *external, internal,* and *eternal*.

This three-dimensional picture is composed of three arenas in which we define success: (1) marketplace standards, or *external*; (2) personal standards, or *internal*; and (3) standards for fulfilling our ultimate purpose, or *eternal*. The first two dimensions are based on where we are in our journey; the third dimension is based on who we're becoming on that journey.

External
The *external* dimension of success is measured by position or possessions. It involves achieving a particular status in life, acquiring a certain amount of material goods, or gaining a measure of power as measured by marketplace perceptions.

We desire external success in order to gain the acceptance of others for personal satisfaction. It's important to feel accepted by others—but striving for it has many drawbacks.

External success rarely makes us feel successful inside. In fact, it often increases our competitiveness, produces guilt, and breeds resentment. It makes competition a constant companion. We compete for positions that other people think we should have. We spin our wheels in frustration as we try to meet unrealistic standards.

To counteract these effects we must open our eyes to see that success, as dependent on external standards, is temporary. We can be a queen today and a scapegoat tomorrow.

Dede, the president of a large temporary service, had worked hard for her position. She excelled all the way up the ladder. Even under fierce pressure from competition, Dede maintained her high standards and would not compromise her values.

But when competitors began taking away several big clients, the board of directors began to view Dede as the problem. Dede later reflected, "I'm the same person I was when I received that recognition. Now I realize they weren't applauding *me*, but what I could do for *them*."

Internal

Internal success is defined by our own standards of what it means to succeed. This dimension can bring benefit or harm depending upon what our criteria are and why they're important to us.

If we're using healthy criteria to qualify success, then being inner-directed will give us a basis of strength in our journey through the marketplace.

If we're measuring success according to unhealthy standards, we may breed troubling patterns such as self-centeredness, self-sufficiency, chronic dissatisfaction, or a compulsive need to prove ourselves. We'll end up with the same emptiness that external success, without internal meaning, can produce.

The challenge in developing an internal success structure is to build it on the right values and perspectives. Once we do, we'll be better able to control our feelings about success. As we use our own criteria for setting the targets we're aiming at—for example, achievement of our Milestones—we will increasingly find contentment in our accomplishments. What others view as successful will fade in importance.

Once you have a healthy internal success system in place, your achievements will become pleasurable fulfillments. They may or may not be considered successful by external standards, but that will no longer be a factor. You'll look at your work more as a labor of love than a labor for approval. You'll find that preoccupation with competition and position gives way to the fulfillment of accomplishing your own goals.

Judy decided when she was young to become a nurse. She went through college at the top of her class. When she entered the nursing field, she found great satisfaction in comforting others and a great sense of accomplishment in meeting needs.

Judy's professional abilities got the attention of the hospital administration. They offered her a management position with higher pay but less patient contact. Judy followed internal signals and declined the offer. "If I'd accepted that position," she explained, "I'd feel like I failed in what I was called to do—be a comfort to hurting people."

Eternal

External and internal definitions provide a two-dimensional representation of success. In order to picture success in its fullest sense, we need the third dimension: *eternal.*

Eternal success is defined by working toward our vision for fulfilling our ultimate purpose. This kind of success does not single out any one element as a criteria for achievement—income, advancement, even personal growth. Instead, it focuses on the process of who we're becoming and why we're striving.

This process is living as God's ambassadors in the marketplace to carry out His plan. As we participate in this process, we become successful in eternal terms. We learn that the significance of our journey lies in God's hands, not in human eyes. If we follow God's leading and don't compromise His principles we will enjoy this journey. What could be more successful than that?

Measuring by the standards of eternal success has been expressed beautifully by Philip Bailey:

We live in deeds, not years; in thought, not breath;
In feelings, not in figures on a dial.
We should count time by heart-throbs. He most lives
Who thinks most, feels the noblest, acts the best.
Life's but a means unto an end; that end . . . God.[1]

A young careerist said to me recently, "I have too much to give up to have a family." In my heart I felt prompted to say to her, "It's hard to know what you have or what you will give up if you're looking to be successful. Success is a starting point, not a stopping point."

We can never give up too much if it's part of God's purpose for our being. To turn our backs on His gracious plan is to step into the chaos of a life that has no eternal dimension.

SUCCESS IS A REFLECTION OF PROGRESS

Now you may be thinking, *Well, okay, I should live by the standards of eternal success. I'm with you there. But that's a pretty lofty concept. What does it look like in practical terms? What really is "successful living"?*

Once I implemented a plan based on purpose and MINI Steps, I perceived success as reaching the destination of Milestones. However, I found that my Milestones were becoming my purpose, instead of landmarks along the way. Now I look at success in broader terms: I'm living successfully as I reach Milestones that mark progress toward turning visions into reality.

Reflection on progress has become a way of judging my success. Just as thinking forward is necessary for Moving In Natural Increments, so reflecting backward is necessary for the feedback that tells me I'm succeeding at what I'm attempting to do.

This kind of reflection gives me the gratification of recognizing Milestones I've reached and seeing how these accomplishments have carried through my purpose and met the needs of others. Each accomplishment is a cause for thanksgiving but not such a lofty feat in the perspective of my journey that I'm tempted to sit back and rest on my laurels.

Living successfully involves prayerful consideration of, and constant progress in, those worthwhile accomplishments that contribute to our overall vision.

Think for a moment about the people you know who truly seem to be successful in their life's work. When you look just under the surface of their lives, most likely you'll discover that they have a strong passion of purpose. They're not targeting "success"; rather, they're aiming at the goal of fulfilling their purpose.

Ralph Waldo Emerson expressed this mindset beautifully in the following poetic lines:

> How do you measure success?
> To laugh often and much;
> To win the respect of intelligent people
>   and the affection of children;
> To earn the appreciation of honest critics
>   and endure the betrayal of false friends;
> To appreciate beauty;
> To find the best in others;
> To leave the world a bit better
>   whether by a healthy child,
>   a redeemed social condition
>   or a job well done;
> To know even one other life has breathed
>   because you have lived —
>   this is to have succeeded.[2]

In this approach to life, success is a result, a reflection of who we are becoming. It's something that occurs as we focus our energies on our driving purpose in life. How freeing this is for those of us who have lived under the tyranny of thinking that we must be "successful." Living successfully really means *living purposefully*.

I opened this chapter by telling you about Renee, the apparently successful woman who discovered that the world's definition of success had a hollow ring to it. I encouraged Renee to develop her own plan of what she wanted to accomplish. She needed to decide what was important to her and what goals were eternally significant.

Renee took me to lunch shortly after she began developing a life plan. Beaming like a child who had just discovered gifts under a Christmas tree, she said, "As you say, I'm 'successing'!" Her grin seemed to stretch even wider as she went on to explain, "I haven't arrived, but I'm on the road again. I know the key is staying on the road to fulfilling my purpose. I discussed my feelings with my husband. I also accepted the fact that I can't change my boss's attitude. Nevertheless, I'm doing the right things according to *my* definition of success. Even more importantly, I believe I'm doing the right thing according to God's definition."

Renee had gone through Consciousness-Raising 101 on successful living. She had become aware that external success in the marketplace is precariously based on contingencies. By drafting a life plan, she grasped anew what was important to her and to those around her. She understood that part of being successful is linking internal desire to external opportunities.

The most important truth for successful living is to remember that we must aim at the target of our purpose. If we shift our aim and make success our target, we forget our purpose for being in the marketplace. Then we're right back where Renee used to be, the sand of our supposed accomplishments sifting through our fingers as we wonder why once we achieve "success" we can't seem to hold on to it.

SUCCESS GUARANTEED

Children's author "Dr. Seuss" has an exuberant way of painting creative word pictures with edifying messages for young and old alike. One of his books, *Oh, the Places You'll Go!*, is a humorous verse on the ups and downs, the rewards and disappointments, of our journey through life. It emphasizes personal initiative in embracing opportunities:

> You have brains in your head. You have feet in your
> shoes. You can steer yourself any direction you choose.
> You're on your own. And you know what you know.
> And YOU are the guy who'll decide where to go. . . .
> Out there things can happen and frequently do to
> people as brainy and footsy as you. And when things
> start to happen, don't worry. Don't stew. Just go right
> along. You'll start happening too. . . . And will you
> succeed? Yes! You will, indeed! (98 and ¾ percent
> guaranteed.)[3]

Is success guaranteed? If so, there are women galore who will rise up and say, "I'd like to cash in on that guarantee!"

We know that life hands us no guarantees that it will happen just the way we want it to. But there is a sense in which success is guaranteed, if we characterize success as *responding to the changing conditions of life by staying on course toward our ultimate purpose.*

We have control over this kind of success. We can achieve it as we focus on where we're going and what we're doing along the way. To use Dr. Seuss's imagery, we all have places to go; things are going to happen "out there" along the way; and with the right responses we can expect a guarantee of success.

Places to Go

To be successful, we must set our sights on where we're going. However, success doesn't depend on where that place is. Success occurs in the *action* of going, not in the *destination*.

Our sense of direction comes clear as we merge our agendas to cut a path for our life journey. Not many of us would pick up a dart and try to hit the bull's-eye while blindfolded. Setting our sights in the marketplace requires that we know what to aim for so we won't hit the wall.

An important part of this planning is that the "place" you target must be *your* place. It can't be someone else's choices for you. *You* must be the architect of your own blueprint. If your plans have been designed by someone else, you will not succeed in working toward your purpose.

Think of how easy it is to surrender our choices under pressure from outside opinions of what it means to be "successful": the homemaker who thinks she has to have a "real job" in order to be a somebody; the stockbroker who went after the lure of the "big time," all the while yearning to be a high school coach; the medical student who wanted to be a nurse but was persuaded by others to "aim higher."

No one is going to waste her life if she looks at success based on eternal values. What place we live, what position we hold, or what potential we have for tomorrow aren't as important as how we put these resources to use in heading down the road of eternal significance.

The writer of the book of Hebrews emphasized the importance of staying on course toward our purpose when he wrote,

> Let us throw off everything that hinders and the sin that so easily entangles, and let us run with perseverance the race marked out for us. Let us fix our eyes on Jesus, the author and perfecter of our faith, who for the joy set before him endured the cross. . . . Consider him who endured such opposition from sinful men, so that you will not grow weary and lose heart.[4]

Most of us are familiar with the story of Helen Keller, the blind and deaf woman who broke through the prison of her limitations and lived her life to the fullest. But not many of us know much about Anne Sullivan, the gifted teacher who empowered Helen Keller's transformation.

As a child raised in a mental institution, Anne was one of the least likely to succeed. But a nurse saw a spark of hope for this little girl, and she took a compassionate interest in her. When the apparently hopeless child was released, Anne had a heart full of compassion to help others. Because someone had seen potential in her, Anne was able to detect potential in Helen Keller and draw it out. Each life that was touched in this remarkable chain of caring went on to touch other lives.

Who was successful — the institutional nurse, Anne Sullivan, or Helen Keller? Each was successful, because *each woman knew what she wanted to do with her life and did it.*

The Things that Will Happen

As we travel through life, things are going to happen to us — some good, some bad. Most of them will be out of our control. But although we can't control events, we can control our response.

If we focus our attention on whether things will turn out the way we want them to, we risk losing our direction. It's been said that there are two things people regret most: (1) not getting what they want; and (2) getting what they want. I've known both these feelings.

When I entered the marketplace, I really had never defined success for myself. The first thoughts of success that I entertained were simply preoccupations with the fear of failure. This fear alone propels more people than do plans for accomplishment.

My "do or die" mindset lasted until I realized that my success didn't depend on bad things not happening. It depended on how I responded when bad things happened.

Accepting our limitations is part of successful living. Another part is judging our success based on our efforts, not our achievements. We must be diligent in our work. But it's the Lord's gift to us to enjoy the *results* of our efforts—"that everyone may eat and drink, and find satisfaction in all his toil—this is the gift of God."5

That covers the things that we *don't* want to happen. What about the things we *do* want to happen? I've often said that it's easier to handle stress than success. Napoleon made a remark to that effect when he commented, "The most dangerous moment comes with victory." Why? Because we get more practice handling the struggles than the achievements.

Success can create chaos faster than you can blink your eyes. Once you're in a "success" mode, you immediately risk becoming a victim of maintaining that status. The expectations rise, and so do the pressures.

What a nice problem to have, you may be thinking. But it's a serious problem just the same. One aspect of it is pride, which is usually lurking around the corner just waiting to make its appearance. Have you ever suffered the excruciating humiliation of puffing yourself up only to have someone come along and deftly prick your bubble? That hot air rushing out through the hole is pride taking a well-deserved fall. When you begin equating success with recognition, the things that happen aren't always what you plan.

At times like these, the right response is *not* to wallow in self-pity or self-condemnation. Instead, we should turn the takedown into a stepping stone for readjusting our sights. Maybe the next time we respond to a successful experience we won't stray so far off the target.

It takes commitment to keep going when the going gets tough. The key is focusing more on how we respond to the things that happen to us than on whether those things are "good" or "bad." We often base our values on calling the "good" things successful and the "bad" things failures. But all of them are proving grounds that can teach us to stay on track—whether we're in the midst of problems or on top of them.

The Assurance of Success

Success gained according to marketplace terms is often bitter-sweet. I've been amazed at how many times I've simultaneously felt fantastic and a failure. Trying to maintain a particular level of success in multiple agendas can keep us coming up short in one or another of them.

When I began working to synchronize my agendas, it became easier for me to eliminate the frustration of not knowing where I stood. The glamor and glitz of success is gone for me, perhaps forever. In its place is the conviction that success lies in having peace in the midst of chaos.

The assurance of success comes when we're concerned more with our method of movement than with how high we climb. Theodore Roosevelt said it well:

> It is not the critic who counts; not the man who points out how the strong man stumbled or where the doer of the deeds could have done better. The credit belongs to the man who is actually in the arena; whose face is marred by dust and sweat and blood; who strives valiantly; who errs, and comes up short again and again, because there is no effort without error and shortcoming; who does actually try to do the deed; who knows the great enthusiasm, the great devotion and spends himself in a worthy cause; who, at the worst, if he fails, at least fails while daring greatly.
>
> Far better it is to dare mighty things, to win glorious triumphs even though checkered by failure, than to rank

with those poor spirits who neither enjoy nor suffer much because they live in the gray twilight that knows neither victory nor defeat.[6]

Our guarantee is not that we will finish at or near the top by marketplace standards, but that we will have the guidance and strength to stay on course.

When we define success as staying on course toward our ultimate purpose, then we can evaluate our performance by comparing what we're doing against the best we can do. Gone are the arbitrary standards and expectations that turn success into a tyrannical dictator. We can look for rewards in long-term results and in knowing that whatever happens, good will come out of it. God himself has guaranteed it.[7]

THE SECRET OF SUCCESS

So often we look at success with eyes that see only the glory of recognized accomplishment. We don't look at the sacrifice and guts it takes to reach levels of attainment.

This shortsightedness can start us off ill-prepared for the journey. Some don't count the cost before making the trip. Others want to make a quantum leap of progress without expending the effort. We can correct our vision with the kind of commitment that Vince Lombardi described when he said, "The price of success is hard work, dedication to the job at hand, and the determination that whether we win or lose, we have applied the best of ourselves to the task at hand."[8]

The secret of success lies in our methods and motives—in setting the right targets. Successful results can be a motivating force. But keep your aim on the target of your driving purpose. Then, when success comes along, don't run from it and don't be controlled by it. Accept it as a responsibility to be a living message to those around you of what it means to live successfully.

Above all, keep your visions, work fervently, and judge your success not on what is happening today but on what the eternal significance will be—and much of that, you will have to leave up to God. Remember that you're responsible for the pursuit of your purpose, not the measurable outcome of your efforts.

I've kept the following poem on my desk and drawn encouragement from it for twenty years. I hope it will also inspire you:

> Often your tasks will be many,
> And more than you think you can do. . . .
> Often the road will be rugged
> And the hills insurmountable, too. . . .
> But always remember, the hills ahead
> Are never as steep as they seem,
> And with Faith in your heart start upward
> And climb 'til you reach your dream.
> For nothing in life that is worthy
> Is ever too hard to achieve
> If you have the courage to try it
> And you have the Faith to believe. . . .
> For Faith is a force that is greater
> Than knowledge or power or skill
> And many defeats turn to triumph
> If you trust in God's wisdom and will. . . .
> For Faith is a mover of mountains;
> There's nothing that God cannot do;
> So start out today with Faith in your heart
> And "Climb 'til Your Dreams Come True"![9]

STAY ON THE COMPLETENESS EDGE

▼▼▼▼▼▼

In the presence of the Lord
there is fullness of joy.[1]

Every time we go to Pebble Beach, I marvel at the breathtaking beauty of this stretch of the Pacific coastline. The awesome power of the water beating up against the shoreline always reminds me of how we can feel secure in the turbulence of life.

The sea washes away the sand that has no firm foundation, but its assault leaves unmoved the magnificent boulders that have been in place for centuries. If anything, they just take on a more luminescent glimmer in the sunlight. How deep their foundations must be in order to prevent them from being swept away by the turbulent current.

Perilous crosscurrents are beating against working women in today's marketplace. Some women seem to stand strong, even against the fierce onslaught of external circumstances. Others are undermined by the force of these currents, little by little.

What kind of foundation can keep us steady, even make us shine a little brighter, when the waves are breaking all around us? What does it take to avoid being swept into the cycles of chaos?

To answer these questions, we must let the truth penetrate our frustrations and disappointments, the overwhelming pressures of everyday life. Then we can learn to stand firm against the

all-consuming power plays of the marketplace. We can discover that God makes His inexhaustible power available to us; we can believe in His love for us; we can trust His design for our lives.

I haven't always been able to do this. Early in my life, chaos became my constant companion. It seemed that before the dust settled on one crisis, another would kick up. No matter how often they came, I was never prepared for them. The foundation of who I wanted to be seemed to be washing away, bit by bit, in the powerful currents of reactions I couldn't seem to correct.

In this book, I've shared with you my search for what it means to be God's woman in God's plan, marketplace style, and how to develop a firm foundation on which to build tomorrow, today. Now I want to focus on the cornerstone of that foundation: the most important part of the plan, which enables us to maneuver successfully through the marketplace.

To talk about this cornerstone I need to go back to my initial search to find a solution to the chaos in my life. The search broke wide open when I found the "completeness edge" —faith in Christ. That faith is what enables me to share with you that victory is possible in the pressures of the marketplace. Otherwise, I would still be a victim of, not an overcomer in, a chaotic environment.

THE COMPLETENESS EDGE

"Staying on the cutting edge" is the vernacular for being one up on the competition. Maintaining this position depends on many variables—degree of expertise, pricing structures, innovative strategies, timing, and so forth. In essence, it's having the right combination, at the right time, in the right place.

The "completeness edge" depends on being in the right relationship with God through Jesus Christ. The Apostle Paul tells us that the fullness of God is in Christ. When we allow Christ to dwell within us, we share in His fullness. In Christ, Paul declares to us, we "have been made complete."[2]

Trusting in Christ gives us the completeness edge: through Christ we have unlimited power and potential. The purpose of

this "edge" is not to give us a competitive advantage, but peace in the midst of chaos, the power of prayer, the assurance of God's promises—everything we need for the life of faith in today's world. Thomas Kelly describes it like this:

> The life that intends to be wholly obedient, wholly submissive, wholly listening, is astonishing in its completeness.
> Its joys are ravishing, its peace profound, its humility the deepest, its power world shaking, its love enveloping, its simplicity that of a trusting child.[3]

Yes, chaos is here to stay; it's a fact of life. But when we trust in Christ, chaos loses its power to throw us off course. We have an anchor that keeps us in place even while the storms rage around us.

For years, I tried to pin the turmoil in my life on others. It seemed I was constantly bombarded with unpredictable, unavoidable, and uncontrollable events. I kept looking for reasons why these events were happening so I could figure out how to make them stop.

But I've since found that it isn't the tides of events that pull me under; it's the way I react to them. This is where the completeness edge makes a profound difference. The best way I know to describe that difference to you is to tell you the story of my own search for peace, happiness, and security.

GROWING UP IN CHAOS

My early years were centered around a humble abode in a small, rural Alabama community. My mother had the awesome responsibility of raising two children as a single parent. Those were the days when jobs for women were limited and wages were meager. The only way Mother could survive the situation at first was to leave my brother and me with my grandparents.

As a child, I could never comprehend how difficult this life must have been for my mother. Nor did I understand the depth of her commitment when she moved my brother and me out of our grandparents' home and in with her in Atlanta. This was a bittersweet change for me. I was brokenhearted about leaving my grandparents but excited about going to the big city.

One of the first problems I ran into after this move was the discovery that Mother did not look at me through the same rose-colored glasses as Granddaddy did. Actually, she had quite a different philosophy of child-rearing. My grandfather had thought that I was perfect and could do no wrong. But Mother thought that children, like canoes, go in the right direction when paddled from the rear. The sudden change from "perfection" to parental authority began my first siege of chaos.

That chaos was not the result of having a single working mother; it was the result of my response to the circumstances. Looking back, I think it started when I began missing the father I had never known. I had always been told that my father had died just before my birth, and I had accepted that news because my grandfather had been there for me. But when Granddaddy was no longer a part of my daily life, acceptance gave way to inquisitiveness.

One weekend while I was visiting my grandparents, I discovered my fatherlessness was due not to death, but to parental choice. The news that my parents had divorced brought my world crashing down around me. When my mother finally gave me a reason why she and my father decided to leave the marriage, it didn't satisfy me.

In the early fifties, divorce was not accepted the way it is today. It carried a stigma that is no longer prevalent. I didn't understand my parents' divorce at the time, and it planted a seed of resentment that ripened into teenage rebellion.

Have you ever been around a rebellious teenager? Can they ever make life miserable! But like many rebellious teenagers, I didn't feel that I was doing anything wrong. My form of rebellion wasn't "hard core"; it revealed itself in a resentful and demanding attitude. I was one of those children who can't accept responsibility for their own actions and therefore try to pin the blame on others.

"Resentment is like racing an emotional motor," the saying

goes: "You use up valuable energy, but you don't get anywhere." During my teenage years, I used up a lot of energy spinning my wheels in the wrong gear. When my brother, Craig, who had been my primary source of strength, left home to attend college, I just revved up my motor of resentment and began looking forward to the day when I too could leave home.

What I really wanted to do was go to college, but it was financially impossible at the time. Since college was not going to be my escape route from home, I had to find a detour.

I made it my top priority to obtain a full-time job and get a place of my own. I was no stranger to work. At a very young age I'd gone to work after school to help meet family needs. But this would be my first exposure to "the exciting world of business."

Just before I graduated from high school, I applied to become a secretary in a sales office. The usual nervousness that accompanies job interviews only increased as my heart did flip-flops over the debonair sales manager who was interviewing me.

I was thrilled when I got the job. Of course I didn't know at the time how this interview would affect the rest of my life. Until this day I still tell that sales manager, "I don't know if you were just a good salesman or I was just an impulsive buyer." Whatever the case, he offered me a lifetime position: I eventually said yes to becoming John's wife. But even this would become another difficult learning experience in my search.

The most important element in my story so far is that my consistent response to situations I had no control over was self-centeredness, caused by resentment and a desire to escape. This always leads to chaos.

TIME OF RECKONING

My husband was the only brother among eight sisters. They thought he could do no wrong, and so he usually got what he wanted. This should remind you of someone else I've just been telling you about. Here we were, chaos attracting chaos—and so perhaps you won't be surprised to hear that our first year of marital bliss had many blizzards.

We managed to weather those early storms, and my hopes rose as John was promoted and we were transferred. I looked forward to the new location as a new start—maybe we would just leave those storms behind us.

Like so many women, I thought that since marriage hadn't made my world perfect, motherhood would bring me the joys I was searching for. But it didn't take long for me to discover that along with the little bundle of joy came not-so-little bundles of diapers and plenty of wake-up calls in the middle of the night. Then the bigger truth sunk in that my child was not there to fulfill *my* needs; I was there to fill *hers*.

Terri did bring new meaning to my life. She also gave me a new perspective on my relationship with my mother. I was so excited when shortly after Terri's birth, Mother relocated to our area. For the first time in years, we were able to enjoy each other. We even found out that we could communicate! For the first time since I was five years old, I felt truly happy.

But that happiness would be short-lived. Chaos reared up again all too soon when we found out that my mother was terminally ill. This began what I call "my year of reckoning."

During the following months, I struggled to be a dutiful wife, a good mother, a competent secretary, and a comforting daughter. Those are big orders for anyone. I was trying to do it all alone, and it was overwhelming.

In February of that year, Granddaddy died. He had been the only father I had ever known. Two months later, Mother passed away. Just when I thought I couldn't stand another loss, I found out I could and would. I had no choice in the matter. Within another two months, my husband and I were separated.

I was left alone as a single parent, desperately needing someone I could depend on. I had never really appreciated the mother I'd had until it was too late. How I longed to retrieve those wasted years!

In my desperation, I spent a lot of time and money I didn't have trying to find a man I'd never seen—my father. I had no idea if he was dead or alive. And if I did get lucky enough to find him, I had no idea whether he would even want to see me.

After running into many dead ends, I realized I was trying to accomplish an impossible task.

As I reflected back on my life during that period of misery, all I could see was pain, rebellion, and frustration. It seemed to rain down on me out of a cloud of resentment that I kept hovering over my life. I had searched in many ways to find peace, happiness, and security. Some of them had given me some temporary satisfaction. Others had given me important additions, such as my daughter. But none had taken care of the chaos within me.

QUIETING THE INNER STORM

Right in the middle of this troubling time I received a letter from a very dear cousin. "Sheila, I'm praying for you," Nan wrote to me. "I only wish that I could give you the faith that I have in God to carry you through."

But of course Nan couldn't do that for me. I would have to discover that faith for myself.

I was not a stranger to religion. Attending church regularly was a primary part of my growing-up years. I even believed the gospel message—that Jesus Christ had died on the cross for the sins of the world, that He had been buried, that He rose from the dead. I considered myself a Christian.

I thought that being a Christian meant believing in God. But my belief hadn't given me "the peace that only God can give" in my heart. Instead, I felt lost in the storm that was raging within me. I couldn't find my way.

A friend suggested that I read the Bible. When I took her up on her suggestion, it was like someone had turned on a light. The Bible said that we are to "seek God" and His righteousness first, above all else in life. For the first time in my life I realized that although I had sought God's *help* many times before, I had never really sought *God*.

I looked further and found that all people were sinners, but God had prepared a way for all people to be forgiven of their sins. Everyone who *believed* in Him and *received* Him would become His children.

It finally dawned on me that becoming a Christian didn't happen just by being raised in a Christian home, or by going to church, or even by believing the right things. To become a Christian I had to *invite* Jesus Christ to come into my life, in a personal act of faith. I had never done this before.

I knelt beside my bed one night and prayed as I had never prayed before. I confessed all the areas of my life in which I could see sin and rebellion. I asked God to forgive me. I asked Jesus Christ to enter my life and be my Savior and Lord. I asked Him to give me the strength to trust and follow Him.

Then I made another request: "God, if it is Your will for John and me to get back together," I prayed, "please help me do what is right until that time comes. If we aren't going to reconcile, I ask You to make me willing to do Your will."

After these prayers I experienced a deep quietness. The raging storm within me had subsided. In the stillness I felt assured that God Almighty was in control of my life. No bells rang, no lights flashed; but I went to bed and slept better than I had in many years. *Finally*, I knew what it was like to be completely at peace.

The next morning brought confirmation of that peace. For the first time in years, I was no longer afraid of "tomorrow." Instead I felt excited about what God was going to do in me, for me, and through me.

The awful burden of guilt rolled off my shoulders as I began to understand the power of God's forgiveness. What a relief to find release from the agonizing weight of those rebellious teenage years!

The most powerful realization of all was that I was no longer alone. I had searched frantically for my father, and now I had found Him—my heavenly Father. And all along, He had been only a prayer away.

After the complications of mounting chaos, I had gotten down to basics. In my prayers I was seeking God, not just His help. I traded in the need for control *of* my life in order to gain control *in* my life. I was still in the midst of chaotic circumstances, but I had the peace of God ruling in my heart.

I had learned that *Christ in me* was the way to become the person I wanted to be. His active presence in my life made me a complete person despite all the losses I had sustained.

THE REALITY BEYOND THE CHAOS

My spiritual awakening did not take me out of the chaos of being a single parent in the marketplace. My husband did not come rushing back to me. I did not get a big raise that made life easier. I had a boss who thought my vulnerable position meant I was fair game to move in on. The conflicts of working in an environment whose standards were not my own became a daily challenge.

In those next two years I grew to love the word *impossible*. That's God's word. He not only began doing the impossible *in* me, but also *for* me. I don't mean that He was another Granddaddy, giving me whatever I wanted (whether it was good for me or not). But He was working in me, changing me into the person He wanted me to be. And that in turn started changing my circumstances.

At that time in my life I thought it was impossible for my husband and me ever to get back together again. I was in Florida and he was in Michigan. But even though so much time had passed, I still hadn't finalized our divorce. I'd waited nearly two years to apply, and everything seemed to put off the finalization for just a little longer — the judge had a personal emergency, there was a fire at the courthouse, I was hospitalized with a sudden illness.

Just a few days before I went into the hospital, I got the shock of my life. John called me and said, "Put off the divorce. Let's try again." As much as I still cared, I was very afraid.

Lying in the hospital bed gave me plenty of time to reflect on John's call. Just as I was thinking about the distances between us, John stuck his head around the door of my room. He'd driven all night from Michigan to be there when I needed him.

When John left to pick up Terri, my prayer of two years before came back to me: *If it's Your will for John and me to get back together, help me do what's right until that time comes.* The time had come. I could not let my fear control me, but trust that even though John and I could fail, God would not.

Our reconciliation wasn't an instant success, but through time and with work God replaced the hurt and heartbreak with a deep love for each other. Growing in my heart was the kind of joy this Scripture passage speaks of:

> The bride belongs to the bridegroom. The friend who attends the bridegroom waits and listens for him, and is full of joy when he hears the bridegroom's voice. That joy is mine, and it is now complete. He must become greater; I must become less.[4]

This passage quotes John the Baptist speaking of Jesus. But when I read it, I knew the joy that John the Baptist referred to. I was the bride whose joy was complete when my husband came back. But even more than that, my real completeness had been accomplished when Christ came into my life. Through the years, I've learned that my control must decrease as His increases.

This experience and those before it taught me that in Jesus, there is a reality *beyond* the chaos. Even when we feel as though we're losing the struggle, Christ is our completeness edge. No loss can take that away from us. When relationships unravel, we need to do what is possible to mend them, work through the disappointments that come with them, and realize we're not alone even when those relationships can't be healed.

GOD WORKING THROUGH US

John and I spent the next few years working on the gap in our relationship. My life was coming together with joy abundantly, and it was topped off by the birth of our son, John III. I had a restored marriage and two precious children—how could I want more?

But something foundational was missing. The void we needed to fill was to make Christ head of our home. I thought it was impossible for my husband ever to take the step of accepting

Jesus Christ as his personal Savior.

This issue became a constant point of prayer for me. As time went on, God showed me that if I would just live my life so my husband could see the love of God through me, and not be a nagging wife, He would do the rest.

Four years after God healed our broken home, I had the privilege of kneeling with my husband at our kitchen table as he asked Jesus Christ to come into his life. It had happened when I least expected it. We'd gone to see the Billy Graham movie *For Pete's Sake*, and John had been able to relate to the characters in it. He saw working men and women in everyday situations, filling the void in their lives by accepting Jesus Christ. He wanted what these people had found, and that night he received it.

Even as I share how God did the impossible in my marriage, I know that others have not had the same experience. It doesn't mean that I did something right or they did something wrong and that's why our prayers have not been answered in the same way. I truly believe the reason God could heal our marriage was that *both* of us were willing. God knew that it could work out for our good and His glory.

Another significant answer to prayer occurred when I asked my husband to join me in searching for my father. John asked me to pray, "God, if it's Your will, help us to find him. If it's not Your will, take the desire to find him away from me."

Once we began working toward the goal of locating my father, the sequence of events that followed staggered my comprehension. After several months I received information on the whereabouts of my father's family in 1945, the year of my birth. The information was twenty-six years old, and I still felt as if we were searching for a needle in a haystack. But on that same day I was able to contact my father's oldest brother, Alex.

Uncle Alex was cautious during our conversation, and I couldn't blame him. I didn't want my father to live in fear that I would turn up unannounced if he chose not to see me. I didn't want my search to damage anyone's life. So I didn't ask where my father was.

My uncle warned me, "Don't expect too much too soon."

"Don't worry," I assured him. "I won't." I knew that God's will would be done, no matter what happened.

Later that same day, John called me to the telephone and said my brother was on the line. I rushed to pick up the phone, excited to tell him all that was happening. The voice on the other end sounded just like my brother, but it was saying, "This is your father."

This is your father kept ringing in my ears. For the first time in my life, I was absolutely speechless. I was also full of joy in knowing that once again God had done the impossible. My father and I eventually developed a wonderful friendship.

In searching for my father, I learned the importance of seeking God's guidance above all and allowing Him to direct my paths. I believe that God's purpose in bringing my father and me together was for Him to work in both our lives. It was God's plan to use me in bringing my earthly father to come to know Him. And it was God's plan to teach me in a deeper way that my identity rests not in my earthly father, but in the Father who made me; in Jesus who died for me; and in the Holy Spirit who lives through me. After all, that's the bottom line of all we do: God working through us to reach others.

CLINGING TO THE FIRM FOUNDATION

We can be confident that our circumstances will work out for our good when we know that we are personally complete in Christ. In a marketplace in which people use others as pawns rather than recognizing their needs and potential, we can find peace in the midst of chaos.

This peace is available to all of us, regardless of position or circumstance. I've worked as both employee and employer, and each has its own brand of chaos. Once during a seminar a woman challenged me, "It's easy for you to talk about the marketplace — you're the boss." I'm sure it seems that way sometimes. But we're all faced with the same decisions for integrity or compromise. We all need to rely on the same power: the power of Christ in us, our completeness edge.

Perhaps this edge is not the kind that the marketplace values as a catapult to the top of our profession. But it puts us in a very important position: the chaos may surround us, but it doesn't have to reign *inside* us.

All of us will struggle not to retaliate when wronged, not to retreat when rejected, not to cover up our own wrongdoing. We will have to work at being courageous in the face of adversity, disappointment, loneliness, and pain.

I urge you to be patient with yourself. But I also want to challenge you to meet those frustrations that barricade the future of your dreams with the only power that can bridge the gap between what you are and what you want to be: the life of Christ in you.

Our completeness edge is the anchor that keeps us steady in the midst of unpredictable relationships. It is the inner guide that keeps us on course toward becoming the person God created us to be. It is the fulcrum that gives us poise in the midst of a competitive environment. When we accept Jesus Christ as Savior and Lord, we will experience the benefits of putting faith into action: prayer, promises, perseverance, and a plan.

Perhaps you've grown discouraged in trying to handle the chaos of life alone. You may be feeling lost and afraid, thinking that there has to be more to life than what you're experiencing. Problems may seem overwhelming.

You don't have to go it alone. What seems impossible to you is not impossible for God. He has a wonderful plan for you. He wants to give you an abundant life—the completeness edge of His love and peace even in the middle of problems that don't go away.

This completeness is only a prayer away. If you want to discover this way of living, take time now to pray. Turn off the answering machine of recorded messages bombarding you from the chaos and begin an intimate conversation with God. Think of prayer in this way:

Prayer is not given as a burden to be borne, or an irksome duty to fulfill, but as unlimited joy and power. It is given that we may "find grace to help us in our time of need," and every time is a time of need. "Pray" is an invitation to be accepted rather than a command to be obeyed.[5]

When you feel the waves pounding against your shore, cling to the firm foundation that will enable you to stand firm in the turbulence of the marketplace. Decide you will be God's woman, staying on the completeness edge. Make Him your Partner in your personal life, your relationships, your work. Let God unleash His power in your life, reveal His love to you, and establish your purpose in His plan.

ACKNOWLEDGMENTS:
A PARTING ENCOURAGEMENT

The process of living, as well as that of writing a book, is much like trying to win an Olympic gold medal while learning the sport at the same time. We want to give it our best shot, yet we have so much to learn.

In order for each of us to become winners amid the very real challenges of our own chaotic conditions, we need the competitive advantage of a passion of purpose. To stay on course, we must be able to communicate clearly what we're trying to accomplish and keep up a consistent, focused effort as we strive for excellence.

You should be aware by now that my desire has been to communicate clearly to you the power of purpose and to ignite within you a desire to move in natural increments with a focused effort toward your purpose.

In recent months, the thought has been vividly reinforced for me that the principles I've been stressing in this book not only work, but they also keep us going even when we're tempted to quit. The need to synchronize agendas, clarify vision, and be driven by purpose rather than immediate circumstances never stops.

A STORY OF THANKS

One of the truths that became even more real to me as I wrote was that opportunities open up as people enter our lives. I've mentioned my beloved friend Peg Haddad. While I was writing this book, she took up residence with the Father. She had been my Marketplace Visionary Person for writing, encouraging me by pointing out insights and abilities she'd noticed in me.

For years Peg would ask me, "Where's the book, Sheila?" When I saw her the week before she died, she challenged me with a sparkle in her eye: "Get off your derriere, put the pencil to the paper, and start pushing!" If she were here today I could say, "Finally, here it is, Peg—and much of it is because of your encouragement."

We all need encouragement. Many of my opportunities to grow that are reflected in this book came from years of nurture received from people who gave words of wisdom, set examples of excellence, and invested personal energy in me.

God seems to time the encouragements to help meet the obstacles. I discovered firsthand the difficulty of leading a business while writing a book, but those synchronization concepts we explored in part 3 came into play for me.

At work, the team at ACI, which has always been an asset, added their value to the process by keeping the business going and me as well. Deanne Campbell spent her summer putting her fingers to the keys as she turned rough draft into clean copy.

In relationships, my family, friends, and colleagues gave cherished encouragement, support, and prayers—and also their understanding that synchronizing my agendas to finish the project meant missing a few steps with each of them. Keeping the pace with me were Donna Gallagher, Joyce Bowman, and my daughter Terri, who served as readers (and rippers). Because of their diverse roles in the marketplace, they helped check to make sure I was hitting the major targets of need for all working women.

This period of my life has also validated the joy of the unexpected—people, places, projects. I expected to work with a publisher and got much more: NavPress teamed up with me to share the vision for meeting the needs of women struggling to create careers without creating chaos. Their group of men and women are supportive and visionary—especially Traci Mullins, my sponsoring editor. Traci is a woman of deep insight who saw the potential for *Beyond Chaos* but went even further to see the potential in me. Her professional guidance from concept to completion is surpassed only by her sensitivity, caring attitude, and ability to make personal connections as God's woman.

These months were also stretching times for my comfort zone. Agility, synchronization, and learning to laugh at myself helped me organize and get through the chaos of my life and of those close to me.

Kathy Yanni, my manuscript editor, and I learned to laugh as we synchronized lives and edited and rewrote copy. She will never know the depth of my gratitude and the sincere respect I have for her tremendous giftedness. Her perceptiveness and wisdom took a manuscript and transformed it into a marketable masterpiece. The insights she brought to the project not only made her an integral part of the process, but added tremendous value to the finished product. We started out this process as two strangers coming together in a passion of purpose. By the time the finishing touches were placed on it, we had formed a bond as two of God's women in God's plan who could say to each other, "My friend."

I'm very sensitive to the fact that there are women who don't feel they have the support systems I do—especially the strength of a husband and partner like John. He's been there in so many of life's challenges as the empowering man God created him to be. His encouragement to become the person God created me to be has kept me going when I wanted to quit. He has lived with me for twenty-seven years as we've learned the true meaning of synchronization, chaos, and purpose. As he has shared with me the good and the bad, he has been my haven in the midst of storm.

John has a son now following in his steps. I will never find the words to express my thanks and love to our son, John III, for the way he unselfishly gave himself to make my vision become reality. Neither of us could have guessed that God would use him not only to touch my life but join the task of writing with me. As my rough draft editor, his effervescent spirit and creative juices kept me going when I thought the words had stopped coming.

To those of you feeling a lack of support, I hope I've told you enough about myself for you to understand that I know what the tough times are like. I feel deeply for working women who are struggling to get beyond the chaos of life to some sense of purpose and meaning that will guide them through. They have been my driving purpose in the writing process.

A CHALLENGE TO PURPOSEFUL LIVING

I hope you've enjoyed reading this book. But even more, I hope you've been inspired by it to start defining for yourself what it means to be God's woman in God's plan. My purpose has been to challenge, encourage, coax, plead with you to direct your life instead of drifting with the tides of chaos. Focus on your "reason for being" and use it as the pivot point of your life to empower you to enjoy the plan God has for you.

In the appendix beginning on page 199, you'll find suggestions for creating a personalized plan using the concepts in this book. I urge you to consider the questions it raises as springboards to developing your own plan for purposeful living.

I know the longing to find peace in the midst of life's multiple demands. My prayer is that you now understand how the passion of purpose can keep you going when others would quit. That even though your problems may not end, you can have peace within and feel that your efforts are making a difference. That you will accept the challenge of creating endless opportunities, counteracting each obstacle, and becoming a catalyst empowering others. That you will take charge with the changes in your life by developing a blueprint for synchronized living that will enable you to use your "completeness edge" — Christ in you — to become God's woman in God's plan throughout your career in the marketplace.

Listen for God's whisper saying to you, "You have a purpose, and I have the plan." As you follow His leading toward that vision of what you were created to become, you may never know what impact your actions are having. But you will know that God loves you, that He has a plan for you, that He wants to give you abundant life—peace, joy, and purpose in the midst of chaos.

God is the Creator of solutions in chaotic conditions. We are to be His workmanship, active in His process. We participate in His solutions as we choose to live beyond chaos as purpose-empowered women. The deepest reward lies in knowing that our ultimate purpose brings glory to God—who has done great things, is doing great things, and is *going* to do great things with our lives.

APPENDIX: CREATING A PERSONALIZED PLAN

It never ceases to amaze me that we will take days, weeks, months, even years to develop the right blueprints for our dream home, plan a vacation, or choose a new wardrobe—but we don't invest the time in developing a picture of what we want to become.

I don't mean that we should create a detailed, all-hours-accounted-for master plan in which we try to cram all the things we're trying to do right. I'm advocating an opportunistic strategy that helps us discover what are the right things we should be doing—and then direct our choices so our actions are more in line with our purpose.

Creating a purpose statement, visions, and Milestones to help keep us Moving In Natural Increments doesn't mean we have to forecast the future and set it in concrete. It simply involves sketching an outline with flexible guidelines for staying on course, making course corrections, and evaluating progress toward our fundamental goals.

As you put in the time and effort to create your own written plan, you'll discover that it's an essential step in taking "AIM" with your life. Too many people dream of plans for their lives without ever taking action on them. A written plan gives you a foundation to build on. It will force you to think carefully about what your purpose and visions should be, evaluate strengths and weaknesses honestly, and provide checkpoints for staying on track or adjusting your course.

I call this written strategy an "AIM Plan," which I've developed as a guide for creating a personalized blueprint for synchronized living. The following sections, which build on the chapters in this book, condense the "AIM Plan" guide into a sequence of questions suggesting how to formulate a purpose statement, paint action-visions, establish MINI Steps, and conduct evaluation and feedback.

Try using a small notebook for writing down your responses and keeping a journal of your progress. Remember that this Appendix is intended to introduce you to creating a personalized plan, not lead you through every single step. Use it to stimulate your thinking and help you start practicing the concepts in *Beyond Chaos*.

THE PURPOSE STATEMENT

The pivot point of your plan must be your purpose statement. The purpose statement should be the outline of who you are, using the roles you play (daughter, friend, wife or mother, employee, colleague, and so on), and should give the direction for what you want to become in those roles. Remember the three dimensions of purpose — created, guiding, and driving — as you answer these questions:

1. What is the purpose you were created to accomplish?
2. What are the character traits or moral values that you want to guide you in the methods you use to pursue your purpose?
3. Based upon your gifts, abilities, and interests, what are the top three major areas in which you are driven to take action to fulfill your purpose?

As an example of a purpose statement, here is one I have developed for myself:

My purpose is to become more like the Master and to make Him more meaningful in my marketplaces.

In the process, to seek a quality of life, becoming all I was created to be without becoming egotistical with every success and overcome with every failure.

♦ To keep the priorities of being a devoted wife, uplifting my husband; and a supportive, non-controlling mother to my children and children-in-love.
♦ With integrity, to be a trustworthy CEO empowering others to profitable business ventures, personal growth, and quality in all areas.
♦ In my relationships, to be a catalyst empowering others — respecting and giving to others without giving up myself.
♦ To be a catalyst in the quality of my life for my community and the contribution made by my church.
♦ To enjoy the process.

INVENTORY OF STRENGTHS AND WEAKNESSES

These questions will help you identify opportunities for growth, gain a healthy self-understanding so you can allocate your resources wisely, and target areas you want to strengthen.

4. What are your three greatest personal strengths?
5. What are your three greatest personal weaknesses/liabilities?
6. In which of these areas would you like to make better use of strengths, or improve weaknesses, for future growth?

ACTION-VISION STRATEGIES

Your visions are personal. They belong to you — they're the passions in which you long to find fulfillment, the desires that God planted in your heart as the unique ways in which your life will bring glory to Him. Painting action-visions gives you the freedom to explore the Big Question: "What do I *want* to happen in my life?"

7. In the area of personal growth, what do you want to happen—physically, emotionally, spiritually? Who do you
   want to become in these areas?
8. In the area of relationships, what do you want to receive
   from others, and what do you want to give to others? Who
   do you want to become in your relationships?
9. In the area of the marketplace, what do you want to happen
   in your work/career? What path would you like to take
   through (in or out of) the marketplace?

MINI STEPS

To start turning your visions into reality, you'll need to formulate specific steps that will enable you to Move In Natural
Increments. The simplest way to plan is to establish short-term,
attainable goals that you have control over. From these you can
formulate Milestones with target dates—weekly, biweekly, or
monthly—which will mark your progress toward your action-
vision. Once you do this for each action-vision, merge your
agendas by scheduling all your Milestones month by month.
Use monthly planning sessions to establish target dates and
evaluate your progress.

For Each Action-Vision
10. What are the opportunities and obstacles you face in turn-
    ing this vision into reality?
11. What are the major steps you need to take in order to fulfill
    this vision? List them in priority order.
12. What are three steps from this list that you can use for
    formulating Milestones in the coming months?
13. What small, decisive steps do you need to take in order to
    reach these Milestones?

For Synchronizing Agendas
14. In the coming month(s), what MINI Steps can you take that
    will move you forward toward your action-visions in your
    varying agendas?

15. What dates should you assign to these steps in order to create a realistic schedule of accomplishment in the coming month(s)?

EVALUATION AND FEEDBACK

Set aside time during monthly planning sessions to review your purpose statement (including the alignment of your three dimensions of purpose), your inventory of strengths and weaknesses, and your action-visions. During these sessions, use the following questions to suggest ways in which you can evaluate your progress in purposeful living.

16. What Milestones have you accomplished in the past month?
17. What Milestones were you unable to accomplish? What were the obstacles?
18. Do you need to adjust or reformulate any of your action-visions?
19. In what areas are you making progress toward excellence instead of survival? In what areas do you need to improve?
20. In what ways do your action-visions open up opportunities for you to be a Catalyst Empowering Others?
21. What adjustments do you need to make in your perceptions of success — external, internal, and eternal?
22. Are you allowing Christ in you to be your completeness edge? Why, or why not?

CREATIVE SOLUTIONS
FOR CHAOTIC CONDITIONS

For further guidance in developing an "AIM Plan" based on the concepts in this book, consult Sheila West's *The AIM Plan: A Blueprint for Synchronized Living*, a package of cassette tapes with accompanying workbook that lead individuals through a step-by-step process in writing their own plan.

To order these materials, obtain information on Sheila West's seminars on personal growth and professional development, or request her to come speak in your area, contact: Sheila West, AIM Concepts, Inc., 15610 South Telegraph Road, Monroe, MI 48161; call 313-243-3454 or FAX 313-243-5710.

NOTES

Chapter 1: Take Hold of Something Incredible

1. Anonymous, quoted in *Motivational Quotes* (n.p.: Great Quotations, 1987).
2. From *Webster's Ninth New Collegiate Dictionary* (Springfield, MA: G. & C. Merriam & Co., 1988).
3. Anne Morrow Lindbergh, *Gift from the Sea* (New York: Random House, 1955), page 46.
4. Colossians 2:6-8.
5. From an episode in Elijah's life, 1 Kings 19:9-13.
6. Mark 1:37-38.
7. John 3:17.
8. John 5:19.
9. John 5:30.
10. John 10:10.
11. John 12:27.

Chapter 2: Adjust Your Own Sails

1. Robert Schuller, quoted in *Motivational Quotes* (n.p.: Great Quotations, 1987).
2. Philippians 1:4-6.

3. Frances M. Ford, *The Pony Engine*, adapted by Doris Garn (New York: Grosset & Dunlap, 1958).
4. Jeremiah 29:11.
5. Adapted from Dennis J. De Haan, *Our Daily Bread* (Grand Rapids, MI: Radio Bible Class, 1990), 18 June.
6. 2 Corinthians 4:1-15.

Chapter 3: Set Your Sights with Action-Vision
1. James Broughton, quoted in *Motivational Quotes* (n.p.: Great Quotations, 1987).
2. Thomas Peters, *Thriving on Chaos* (New York: Alfred Knopf, 1988), page 403.
3. Jack Nicklaus with Ken Bowden, *Golf My Way* (New York: Simon & Schuster, 1974), page 79.
4. Charles Swindoll, *Living Above Mediocrity* (Dallas, TX: Word Publishing, 1989), pages 94-95.
5. See Proverbs 14:6, 10:13, 14:33, 15:14, 17:24, 19:25.
6. Romans 12:11, KJV.
7. Proverbs 20:5.
8. Psalm 111:10.
9. Proverbs 3:5-6.
10. Proverbs 14:29.
11. See Philippians 3:12-14.

Chapter 4: Take Care of Yourself
1. Orisen Swett Marden, quoted in *Motivational Quotes* (n.p.: Great Quotations, 1987).
2. Psalm 46:10.

Chapter 5: Nurture Your Relationships
1. Proverbs 27:17.
2. Robert A. Raines, quoted in *Improving Your Serve*, by Chuck Swindoll (Waco, TX: Word Publishing, 1981), pages 94-95.
3. Ecclesiastes 4:9-10.
4. Isaiah 40:29,31.
5. Psalm 27:10.

Chapter 6: Take Charge with Change in the Marketplace

1. Marie Dressler, in *The Great Business Quotations*, compiled by Rolf B. White (Secaucus, NJ: General Publishing Co., Lyle Stuart, 1986), page 242.

Chapter 7: Sync or Sink: Integrating
Your Agendas with MINI Steps

1. Earle Nightingale, in *Motivational Quotes* (n.p.: Great Quotations, 1987).
2. John Welch, "Today's Leaders Look to Tomorrow," *Fortune*, 26 March 1990, page 30.
3. John W. Gardner, *Self-Renewal* (New York: W. W. Norton & Co., 1981), page 7.
4. Victor Hugo, quoted in *The Great Business Quotations*, compiled by Rolf B. White (Secaucus, NJ: General Publishing Co., Lyle Stuart, 1986), page 123.

Chapter 8: Trade Survival for Excellence

1. John Ruskin, quoted in *Motivational Quotes* (n.p.: Great Quotations, 1987).
2. Quoted by Neal C. Johnson in *The Bible in Business*, compiled by Ron Jenson (Sisters, OR: Questar Publishers, 1989), page 19.
3. Anonymous, "Don't Quit."
4. David C. Needham, *Birthright* (Portland, OR: Multnomah Press, 1978), page 120.

Chapter 9: You Can Influence Others
Through C.E.O. Leadership

1. Philippians 2:14-15.
2. John Naisbitt and Patricia Aburdene, *Reinventing the Corporation* (New York: Warner Books, 1986), page 242.

Chapter 10: Success—Hitting the Right Targets

1. Philip James Bailey, quoted in *I Quote*, edited by Virginia Ely (Old Tappan, NJ: Fleming H. Revell, 1947).
2. Ralph Waldo Emerson, quoted in *The Quest for Character*, by

Charles Swindoll (Portland, OR: Multnomah Press, 1987), page 26.
3. Dr. Seuss, *Oh, the Places You'll Go!* (New York: Random House, 1990).
4. Hebrews 12:1-3.
5. Ecclesiastes 3:13.
6. Theodore Roosevelt, quoted in *Becoming: Your Self in the Making*, by Calvin Miller (Old Tappan, NJ: Fleming H. Revell, 1987), page 133.
7. See Romans 8:28, 2 Corinthians 1:21-22.
8. Vince Lombardi, quoted in *Motivational Quotes* (n.p.: Great Quotations, 1987).
9. Helen Steiner Rice, *Climb 'til Your Dreams Come True.*

Chapter 11: Stay on the Completeness Edge

1. Psalm 16:11.
2. Colossians 2:8-10.
3. Thomas Kelly, *A Testament of Devotion,* quoted in *Ordering Your Private World,* by Gordon MacDonald (Nashville, TN: Thomas Nelson, 1988), page 149.
4. John 3:29-30.
5. Anonymous, in *Prayer: Beholding God's Glory* (Colorado Springs, CO: NavPress, 1989), page 13; adapted from *The Kneeling Christian* (Grand Rapids: Zondervan, 1971).